THE QUEEN'S COMPANION BOOK

RULE YOUR THRONE: OWN YOUR QUEENDOM

By Nicole B. Gebhardt
AUTHOR-SPEAKER-COACH-REIKI MASTER

A DEDICATED
NOTES SPACE

A DEDICATED
NOTES SPACE

A DEDICATED NOTES SPACE

A DEDICATED NOTES SPACE

A DEDICATED NOTES SPACE

A DEDICATED NOTES SPACE

A DEDICATED NOTES SPACE

A DEDICATED NOTES SPACE

A DEDICATED NOTES SPACE

A DEDICATED
NOTES SPACE

Notes

Nicole B. Gebhardt

Speaking, Workshops, retreats, Private Coaching, and VIP Reiki

www.NicoleBGebhardt.com

QUEENS SPEAK

A Podcast Series
Hosted by Nicole with Special Guests

For the Empowerment of Female Entrepreneurs, Leaders, and Professionals

Learn More by Visiting and Signing Up at
www.NicoleBGebhardt.com

Books

By Author Nicole B. Gebhardt

Related to Pregnancy & Infant Loss

Broken Wings Broken Dreams

Taking Flight After Infant Loss and Miscarriage: A Mother's Journey to Live Again

Sign up for updates and news at www.NicoleBgebhardt.com

The Healing Cocoon Companion Book

Emergence After Pregnancy and Infant Loss

Sign up for updates and news at www.NicoleBgebhardt.com

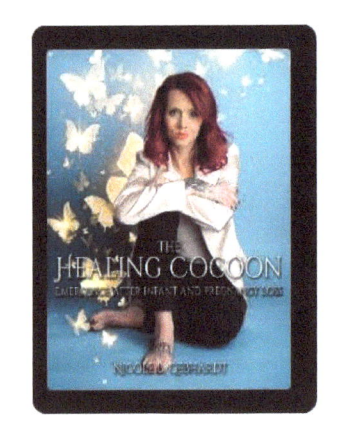

Turning Pain into Purpose

RELATED RESOURCES

A Queen Saves Herself: A Story of Transformation and Triumph

By Nicole B. Gebhardt

Learn about Nicole's memoir and sign up at www.NicoleBGebhardt.com

The Worthy Femme - For Professional Women to Heal & Succeed

Join us and become part of an exclusive and private community of women supporting women

www.facebook.com/groups/nicolegebhardt

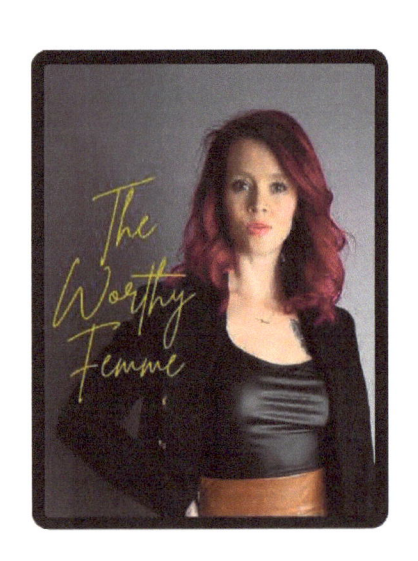

RULE YOUR THRONE
OWN YOUR QUEENDOM

CHECKLIST
PART III

- ✓ Know you are Enough

- ✓ Set your intentions for the day and FOCUS!

- ✓ Write five positive affirmations about YOU

- ✓ Choose to live in the moment

- ✓ Send five texts to friends, family, and others telling them how special they are

- ✓ Let out Pain. Let in Happiness

- ✓ Wake up in Gratitude & go to sleep with gratitude in your heart

- ✓ Do Mirror Work giving yourself compliments

- ✓ Do at least one thing for yourself each day

- ✓ Shift self-doubting & negative thoughts to a positive mindset

- ✓ At the end of the day, choose the best thing that happened and give thanks

- ✓ Be confident, powerful, and unapologetically you

RULE YOUR THRONE

OWN YOUR QUEENDOM

CHECKLIST PART II

- ✓ Prioritize Sleep and Stop Insomnia
- ✓ Visualize and Meditate
- ✓ Let Go and Let God
- ✓ Start your Day and Lead with Your Goals
- ✓ Take Better Care of your Physical and Mental Health
- ✓ Let out Pain, Let in Happiness

- ✓ Turn your Pain into Purpose
- ✓ Mourn your Losses
- ✓ Allow yourself to be Happy
- ✓ Master your Emotions
- ✓ Identify Emotional Triggers
- ✓ Be your Greatest Cheerleader

RULE YOUR THRONE
OWN YOUR QUEENDOM

CHECKLIST

- ✓ Build Self-Awareness
- ✓ Start living and stop numbing
- ✓ Fill up before pouring out
- ✓ Discover core-desired feelings
- ✓ Amplify Self-Love
- ✓ Eliminate Energy Vampires

- ✓ Establish Healthy Boundaries
- ✓ Create more peace
- ✓ Design an action plan for your best life
- ✓ Encourage more support in your life
- ✓ Make positive changes
- ✓ Empower yourself with affirmations

OWN YOUR QUEENDOM

MORE THAN GOLD

WORTHINESS

RULE YOUR THRONE

SELF-DIRECTION & CONTROL

EMPOWERMENT

WEAR YOUR CROWN

POWER AND PURPOSE

IDENTITY

SECRETS UNLOCKED

YOU HAVE THE KEYS!

Your Coronation

You have done the hard work participating in this deep dive of preparing yourself to live your best life. It has, undoubtedly, been painful, insightful, and rewarding. I hope it's been healing and transforming, as well.

Visualize yourself now accepting the crown that is bestowed upon you. You have the power...you always did. You simply needed to believe it, see it, and reclaim it. Take the special vow of being true to your authentic self every day.

With the crown, comes not only the service to yourself to be your true and unique self but also to serve as a leader to others-your family, friends, profession, divine purpose, and community. The bestowal of your crown is also a responsibility to invest your gifts, talents, and services to others. I encourage you to join us.

Together, we can change not only ourselves but the world. And that is the truly formidable power of Queens!

CONCLUSION

Coronation of a Queen

YOU HAVE EVERYTHING INSIDE TO STEP INTO YOUR POWER. REMIND YOURSELF EVERY DAY. HEAL, TRANSFORM, AND EMBRACE YOUR UNIQUE GREATNESS!

Step-by-Step Summary
Worth More Than Gold

1 Imperfect and Enough

2 Banish Perfectionism

3 Overachiever Recovery and Recalibrate the Balance

4 Be Unapologetically You

Banish Perfectionism + Recalibrate Balance and the need to Achieve + Be your Authentic Self = You are More valuable than Gold

"WHEN YOU UNDERVALUE WHO YOU ARE, THE WORLD WILL UNDERVALUE WHAT YOU DO AND VICE VERSA."

—SUZE ORMAN

Remind yourself of your worth Part IV

Reinforce that your worth is not determined by what you do or achieve. It comes from who you are and cannot be taken away from you. Write as many things as you can to describe your value as a person.

Remind yourself of your worth Part III

Seek out supportive relationships. Surround yourself with people who value and respect you for who you are rather than what you do. Supportive relationships will boost your confidence in your personal worth. What kind of support do you need and where will you find it?

Engage in activities that bring you joy. Doing things that bring you joy, fulfillment, connection, and remind you of your value. What do you enjoy and can commit to doing more of it?

Remind yourself of your worth Part II

Focus on your powers and positive qualities (who you are, not who you are not).
We all have talents and special attributes that make us unique. Take the time to reflect on yours and remember that they're part of what makes you valuable and worthy.
What did you discover about your powers and purpose (See Chapter One)?

Set boundaries. It's important to set boundaries and ensure that you are taking care of yourself and your needs. This will encourage you by taking control of your life, reminding you of your own worth, and valuing yourself as an individual. Where do you need to improve your boundaries?

HOW TO REMIND YOURSELF OF YOUR WORTH

Practice self-compassion. Treat yourself with kindness and understanding, just as you would with someone you love. Remember that everyone makes mistakes and has setbacks. Try to be gentle with yourself when things don't go as planned. In what areas do you need to give yourself more compassion?

MORE VALUABLE THAN GOLD

Your worth as a person is not tied to your
achievements or what you do for others.
Your worth comes from who you are as a person.
It is not dependent on external factors.
It is not determined by the opinion of others.
Value, protect, and feverently guard your worth!

Appreciate Your Uniqueness

There's not another woman out there like you. You have a purpose. You are here to make a difference. Love yourself just as you are. Your authentic self has power. Celebrate and embrace the strength and value of being "one of a kind." Write as many things as you can to describe your uniqueness.

"What makes you different or weird — that's your strength."

– Meryl Streep

BE UNAPOLOGETICALLY YOU!

Being "unapologetically yourself" means that you are confident in who you are and are not afraid to be yourself...even if it's not in line with societal norms or what others may expect of you.
It means that you are willing to be true to yourself and your values.

Be true to yourself. Don't try to be someone you're not or do things against your values just to please others.

Stand up for yourself. Don't be afraid to assert yourself. Speak up. You have the right to your own opinions, respectfully expressed.

Don't apologize for being YOU.

Surround yourself with supportive people who accept and support you for who you are.

YOUR AUTHENTIC SELF

WHAT CAN YOU DO TO BE MORE OF YOUR AUTHENTIC SELF?

RECALIBRATING YOUR BALANCE & NEED TO ACHIEVE

- Enjoy the adventure instead of focusing so much on the result.
- Appreciate where you are now as opposed to being only future-driven.
- Take breaks and manage the tasks at hand reasonably.
- Accept who you are along with the uniqueness and cumulative advantages of your life experiences, education, and authentic perspective.
- Don't glorify overworking, sacrifice, burnout, and a lack of sleep.
- Take time for relationships. Money and fame never replace people.
- Celebrate micro-wins. Small victories and non-work accomplishments are just as important. Redefine success.
- Let go and be happy. Trust the process.

Overachievement Self-Reflection Part II

Do you achieve because you are looking for something else to make you feel good about yourself, because you want others to see your value, or you love how it feels to do your best? Why?

When you meet your goal do you feel a deep sense of accomplishment and satisfaction or do you feel anxious and stressed immediately looking for another goal to achieve?

What sounds most true to you? I have high expectations for myself when it comes to accomplishments and performance OR I feel a constant need to prove myself to others?

OVERACHIEVER SELF-REFLECTION

As a child, WHO made you feel pressure to achieve and accomplish above and beyond?
What are your motivations for your goals now?

Are you driven primarily by external motivations like approval, recognition, or winning? Or are you driven primarily by internal motives such as personal satisfaction or other?

Do you feel aligned or at odds with your self-initiated goals? Which goals aren't in alignment?

Do you rely on your overachieving to cope with stress or do you have other ways to alleviate stress?

OVERACHIEVER RECOVERY

A relentless drive to excel and prove yourself can create substantial imbalance in your life. Physical and mental health problems may occur, as a result.

Over-achievement often stems from feelings of insecurity and inadequacy. Accomplishment can act as a drug that distracts from the pain of not being enough. Overachievers are rarely satisfied for long.

Once you accomplish a goal, you begin to look for the next challenge or rush. You continue to raise the bar higher, often in an attempt to fill the void created from a lack of self-esteem. This precipitates an insatiable cycle with little sense or purpose. And it may be why you feel burned out and continue to grind while enviously watching others enjoy a more balanced life. It can be very tough to get out of this chronic cycle and regain your well-being. Fortunately, overachievement is not a characteristic we are born with but is instead developed. Thus, it is entirely possible to have peace and fulfillment apart from achievement.

OVERCOME PERFECTIONISM

There's a tremendous amount of pressure to be perfect from numerous sources. The pressure can be self-directed, socially-prescribed, or other-oriented perfectionism. Consider the source and analyze where this is coming from for you. There's a major difference between achievement-goal driven, high performance-motivated, and success-determined vs. perfectionism. It's the extreme and unreasonable that prompt anxiety, stress, and unhealthy behaviors. If however you're feeling you must be perfect- be aware of these tendencies.

How can you overcome the unreasonable and destructive expectations to be perfect? Examine the reasonableness of your goals, the true importance of them, and how they actually impact you, others involved, and your well-being. Focus on the positives. Concentrate on your uniqueness rather than using others as a standard. Be kind and give yourself grace. Learn how to receive and handle constructive criticism, suggestions, and insights from others. Lower the pressure you put on yourself. Acknowledge the accomplishments you've made. Practice gratitude and celebrate the wins, small ones included. See what benefits you receive with your time, relationships, and self-esteem when you're not expecting perfection. Enjoy the "happy accidents" that occur when you aren't controlling the unattainable standards of perfectionism.

Kintsugi is the Japanese art of putting broken pottery pieces back together with gold — built on the idea that in embracing flaws and imperfections, you can create an even stronger, more beautiful piece of art. Know you are a masterpiece. You are imperfect. You are enough-in fact, more than enough. You are beautiful as you are.

"THINK LIKE A QUEEN.

A QUEEN IS NOT AFRAID TO FAIL.

FAILURE IS ANOTHER STEPPING STONE TO GREATNESS."

— OPRAH WINFREY

In what areas do you struggle with expectations of perfectionism?

What do you fear will happen if you're not perfect?

IMPERFECT AND ENOUGH

"No matter what I do and how much I haven't done-
I am ENOUGH."

PERFECTION IS OFTEN THE PATH TO DEPRESSION, ANXIETY, ADDICTION, AND STAGNATION.
PERFECTION IS FREQUENTLY OTHER-FOCUSED: "WHAT WILL THEY THINK?"

"Perfectionism is a self-destructive and addictive belief system that fuels this primary thought:

If I look perfect, and do everything perfectly, I can avoid or minimize the painful feelings of shame, judgment, and blame."

— BRENÉ BROWN

WORTH MORE THAN GOLD

IMPERFECT AND ENOUGH

OVERACHIEVER

RECOVERY

UNAPOLOGETICALLY YOU

CHAPTER TWELVE

Worth More Than Gold

IMPERFECT AND ENOUGH

OVERACHIEVER RECOVERY

Rise above your need to prove and achieve in order to feel worthy

STEP-BY-STEP SUMMARY RELATIONSHIP REALM

1 SELF-LOVE FIRST

2 OWN YOUR STORY

3 BUILD INTIMACY

4 LOVE LANGUAGE FLUENCY

SELF-LOVE + OWN YOUR STORY + INTIMACY + LOVE LANGUAGE FLUENCY =
THE LOVE & SUPPORT YOU NEED

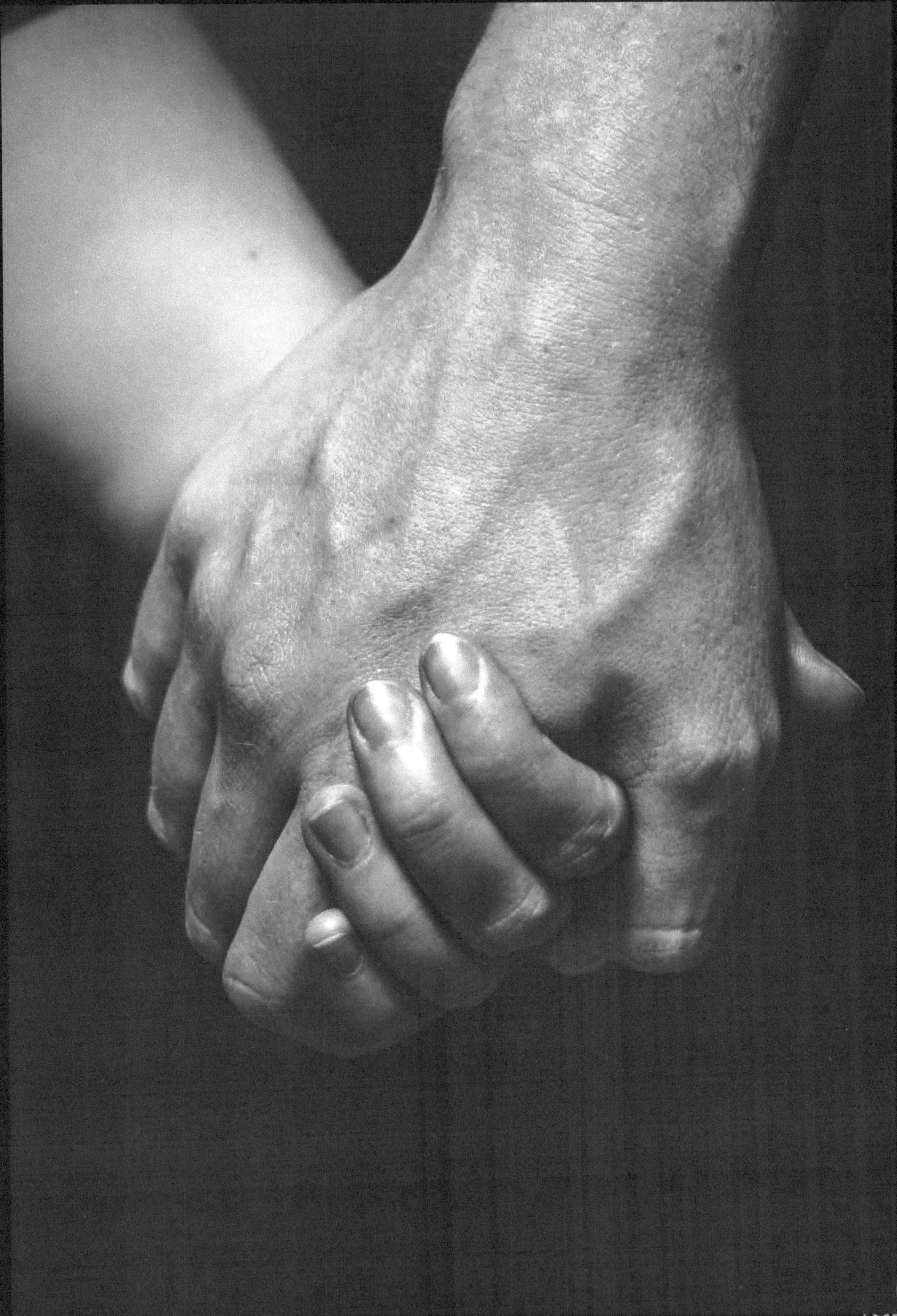

JOURNALING PROMPTS

What do I hope my partner will do differently?

What can I commit to and take action in improving our relationship?

What can I do to encourage my partner's acts to improve our relationship?

JOURNALING PROMPTS

What did I do or say that caused problems between us?
_____
_____
_____
_____

What did they do or say that caused issues between us?
_____
_____
_____
_____

What can I do to make our relationship better?
_____
_____
_____
_____

JOURNALING PROMPTS

What intimacy have I given today? (Physical, sexual, emotional)

What intimacy have I received today? (Physical, sexual, emotional)

What nice things did they say or do to make me feel loved?

DAILY RELATIONSHIP REFLECTIONS

Relationships are hard work! Damn hard. They take daily and serious effort. Use the following Journal Prompts to build a stronger foundation in your relationship or answer the questions as a stand-alone activity.

Reflect on how much you are GIVING and RECEIVING to one another boosting your accountability, gratitude, and intentions to strive for the very best!

LEARN TO SPEAK LOVE

A MUTUAL UNDERSTANDING OF EACH OTHER'S LANGUAGE CREATES THE STRONGEST CONNECTION

WORDS OF AFFIRMATION	Communication is necessary Say what the person is doing well Thanks and Congratulations are important Say "I love you" often Compliment Leave encouraging notes Text special notes
PHYSICAL TOUCH	Hugs and cuddling Non-Sexual touch Kiss hello/goodbye/good morning/night Hand-holding Slow Dancing Together Massage, Caressing
GIFTS	Small gifts often Gifts with thought and care Unexpected gifts and surprises Celebrate accomplishments with gifts Pretty packaging Know what is liked and not liked
ACTS OF SERVICE	Small acts of service Open doors and carry things Cleaning, chores, errands Something nice to save time, relieve stress and simplify life Show appreciation with small acts Volunteer and do charitable acts together
QUALITY TIME	Make time for discussions, dates, vacations together Be 100% present Be a good listener One on one time intentional and unintentional Do chores, hobbies, activities together

LOVE LANGUAGE FLUENCY

THE FIVE LOVE LANGUAGES

WORDS OF AFFIRMATION — 1

GIFTS — 3

PHYSICAL TOUCH — 5

ACTS OF SERVICE — 2

QUALITY TIME — 4

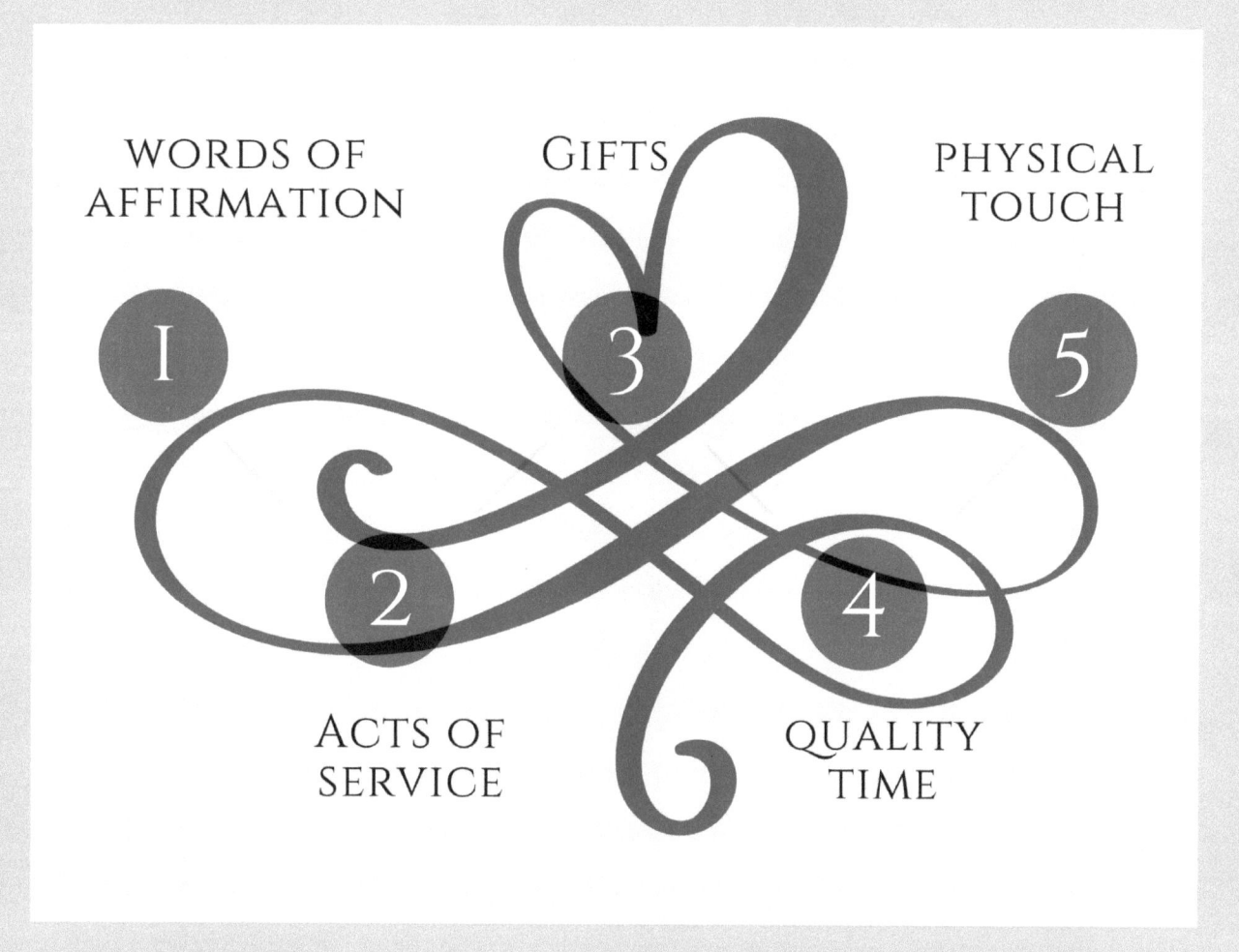

Many of you are aware of the five love languages and have already determined your individual categorization. But how does your language factor into your communication in relationships? You may indeed "speak" your love language quite fluently. However, have you determined the other person's language and do you speak their language, as well? Do you become upset, frustrated, irritated, or give up when someone doesn't know or speak your language? Have you experienced "showing" another person love and them not understand that it is love you are communicating or vice versa?

CHAPTER TEN

Tower of Health

COMMAND YOUR PHYSICAL HEALTH

GUARD YOUR MENTAL HEALTH

INCREASE YOUR WELL-BEING BY TAKING CONTROL OF YOUR PHYSICAL AND MENTAL HEALTH

Six Pillars of Intimacy

Mental Intimacy

Enriching Discussions
Sharing Ideas
Planning
Reading Books

Action Plans

_____
_____
_____
_____
_____

Emotional Intimacy

Vulnerability
Listening and Being Heard
Verbal & Nonverbal Communications
Expressing Needs

Action Plans

_____
_____
_____
_____
_____

Physical Intimacy

Nonsexual Touch
Interpersonal Connection
Hugs
Cuddling
Kissing
Massage
Eye Contact

Action Plans

_____
_____
_____
_____
_____

SIX PILLARS OF INTIMACY

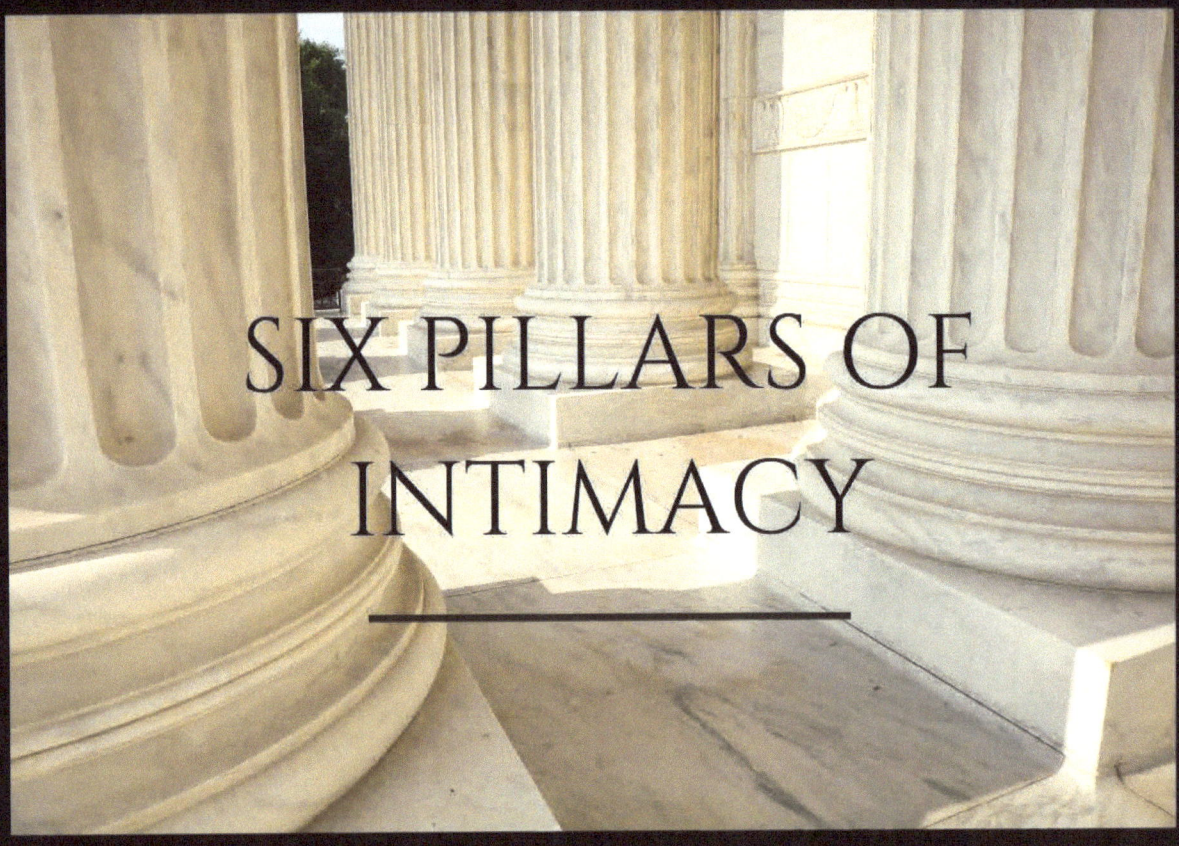

"Intimacy is not something that just happens between two people; it is a way of being alive.

At every moment, we are choosing either to reveal ourselves or to protect ourselves, to value ourselves or to diminish ourselves, to tell the truth or to hide.

To dive into life or to avoid it.

Intimacy is making the choice to be connected to, rather than isolated from, our deepest truth at that moment.

-Geneen Roth

OWN YOUR STORY

I now see how owning our story and loving ourselves through that process is the bravest thing that we will ever do.
—Brené Brown

BE BRAVE to love yourself throughout the trials and tribulations of your life.
One day you will tell your story of how you overcame what you went through and it will be someone else's survival guide.

BODY POSITIVITY AND SELF-LOVE

As women, we are our worst critics. We focus on what is wrong with us instead of what's right. As Lizzo said, "I believe we can save the world if we first save ourselves..." and that begins as she noted, with body positivity and self-love. No matter what your size, age, or physical characteristics, we are all beautiful. When you truly love yourself, you activate your power and serve your purpose.

When I transformed my life, I transformed my body. I felt good again. I ate better. I gave up alcohol. I had the energy and drive to exercise...Eighty pounds lighter and it came after I made myself a priority. I fell in love with myself. But you need to love yourself now not until and when you've achieved your goals. Through self-love, my world opened up and so did my heart. Ask yourself RIGHT NOW what do you love about your body?

Honor your body. Take care of it. Show love to it. Your body is the vessel that holds the passions and gifts that you were born with to give to humanity and yourself. Today, promise me you'll do something nice for it. List one you'll do:

SELF-LOVE COMES FIRST

SELF-ACCEPTANCE
Let go of the need to be perfect and release unrealistic standards. BE PERFECTLY YOU. Know your purpose and what you offer the world. Don't try to be someone you are not. Your only responsibility is to be whom you were designed to be. You were made to fulfill a role that only you can fulfill. Become your best self.

BE PRESENT AND LIVE FOR TODAY
Let go of constantly thinking of the past or future. Learn to be present every day. You have no control over the past or the future. NOW is all that matters. Make it count. When you live in the present, it simplifies and allows loving yourself and others easier.

LET GO AND LET GOD
You cannot control what happens to you but you can always control how you respond. Trust that everything in life is happening for you and not to you. Give God what you cannot understand. Embrace the freedom of peace, knowing you are held safely in God's plan for you.

THINK POSITIVE THOUGHTS
Practice gratitude and ensure your thoughts are positive. You have 100% control over what you think so always be your biggest cheerleader. Do not love yourself with ego but with pure acceptance.

CREATE AN ENVIRONMENT TO GROW AND BECOME
Nothing on earth can grow without the right environment. You must understand what you need to thrive and design that environment for yourself with solid boundaries and self-control. Develop the discipline to have a healthy lifestyle and manage money wisely. Invest your time with people who encourage, accept, and uplift you.

STAY EMPOWERED
Self-care is imperative to self-love. You must take care of your body, mind, and soul. When you care for yourself, you will be empowered to serve others. You cannot give from an empty cup. Fill up so you can pour out. Fuel your body with nutrition; prioritize sleep; and exercise regularly. Take time to connect with God and with yourself every day. Nourish your mind with goodness. Encourage yourself and others with words of affirmation.

RELATIONSHIP REALM

INVITE LOVE

NURTURE INTIMACY

SELF-LOVE FIRST

CHAPTER ELEVEN
Relationship Realm

INVITE LOVE AND NURTURE INTIMACY

SELF-LOVE

CLEAR INTIMACY BLOCKS AND INVITE THE LOVE AND SUPPORT YOU NEED AND DESIRE

Step-By-Step Summary Tower of Health

1 TAKE CONTROL

2 ENGAGE IN THE POWER OF MOVEMENT

3 BUILD HEALTHY HABITS

4 TRACK AND SUCCEED IN NEW HABITS

Command your physical health + Guard your mental health =
Increase in Your well-being for a full life

7 DAY
HABIT TRACKER

KEEPING TRACK OF YOUR HABITS CAN HELP YOU STAY ON COURSE AND ACHIEVE YOUR GOALS.

WEEK OF: _____

HABIT	S	M	T	W	T	F	S
01	○	○	○	○	○	○	○
02	○	○	○	○	○	○	○
03	○	○	○	○	○	○	○
04	○	○	○	○	○	○	○
05	○	○	○	○	○	○	○
06	○	○	○	○	○	○	○
07	○	○	○	○	○	○	○
08	○	○	○	○	○	○	○
09	○	○	○	○	○	○	○
10	○	○	○	○	○	○	○
11	○	○	○	○	○	○	○
12	○	○	○	○	○	○	○

WHAT SABOTAGED ME?

HOW CAN I IMPROVE?

REWARD/CELEBRATE

HOW TO MAKE NEW HABITS STICK

PLACE CUES AROUND TO REMIND YOUR BRAIN OF YOUR NEW INTENTION

Provide your brain a cue to remind you to perform the new habit. When you feel any resistance, acknowledge it, and do the new habit anyway! Focus your attention on the reward as you do it. Cues are alarms, notes to self, objects, pictures, visuals, etc

LAYER YOUR NEW HABIT ALONGSIDE AN ESTABLISHED AND REGULAR HABIT

There are actions you already habitually do like morning coffee, teeth brushing, and bedtime routines. Layer your new habit with one you do so the cue will align times, places, and acts of the new habit during the established habit. This will increase your success in implementing your new habit.

IDENTIFY THE REWARD

When you want to create a brand new habit, be clear on the reward you will gain and do everything you can to create a desire for that reward. Visualize and experience what that reward will give you to stimulate your motivational muscles. Make the incentive strong enough to overcome the resistance you will face when you try to do something new.

COMMIT TO THREE NEW HABITS TO ADD TO YOUR ROUTINE. LIST HERE:

HEALTHY HABITS

SCHEDULED TIME OF EXERCISE

BIGGEST OBSTACLE TO EATING HEALTHY

ONE THING YOU CAN ADD OR ELIMINATE FOR YOUR HEALTH

HOW CAN YOU HOLD YOURSELF MORE ACCOUNTABLE

IF YOU SPLURGED, WHAT EXTRA BALANCE OR ACTION CAN YOU TAKE?

WHAT WILL YOU WRITE ON THE MIRROR FOR ENCOURAGEMENT?

MANTRAS TO SAY FOR ENCOURAGEMENT WHILE WORKING-OUT

ONE THING YOU CAN DO DAILY TO ADD MORE SELF-CARE IN YOUR LIFE

EXERCISE WHEN YOU HAVE A MENTAL HEALTH CHALLENGE

Beginning an exercise routine and staying motivated can be difficult. But when you are suffering with your mental health, it can seem extremely arduous. Here are a few tips to overcome the obstacles:

START SMALL
Don't feel you need to do an hour workout. Simple stretching each morning for a week is a good start. Walk a block instead of a mile. Begin with 5-7 minutes of basic cardio. Numerous apps and YouTube videos can guide you with short and effective programs.

MAKE EXERCISE ENTERTAINING OR PLAYFUL
Layer on pleasure alongside your scheduled exercise. Work out with a friend. Socialize. Listen to your favorite podcast or music. Create a motivating playlist. Sing! Dance; play a sport; bicycle; rollerblade; swim; horseback ride. Have fun!

DOUBLE DUTY PRODUCTIVITY
Count some of your movement as double rewards. Use your chores as moving time. Vigorous household tasks can get the heart pumping. Walk the dog. Play with your children. Romantic moonlight walks and sex with your partner also burns calories!

REWARD YOUR EFFORTS
When you show up, do good things for your body and soul. Take a nap, soak in the tub, read, flip through a magazine. Celebrate your wins...even the micro ones.

POWER OF MOVEMENT

MOVEMENT IS "MEDICINE"

"Movement is a medicine for creating change in a person's physical, emotional, and mental state."-
Carol Welch.

Evidence has shown that people who exercise regularly tend to be resistant to many mental health issues.

Again, the brain/mind and body connection is apparent.

BENEFITS OF EXERCISE

- Can assist to balance our natural chemicals and hormones
- Reduces blood pressure
- Connects you with your body
- Builds strength and flexibility
- Greater endurance
- Enjoyable form of recreation
- Part of a healthy routine and form of self-care, self-love and stress-relief
- Adds variety to your life and relationships
- Boosts self-esteem
- Lose weight and increase muscle

Loving warning to OVERACHIEVERS:
Watch that your need to exercise isn't obsessive, controlling, injury-inducing, or takes priority over everything and everyone. Be sure the calories you burn don't determine what you are allowed to eat. If this sounds like you, be cautious you're not using exercise to cope rather than for self-care

TOWER OF HEALTH

TAKE CONTROL
COMMAND YOUR
PHYSICAL HEALTH
GUARD YOUR
MENTAL HEALTH

CHAPTER TEN

Tower of Health

Command Your physical health

Guard your mental health

INCREASE YOUR WELL-BEING BY TAKING CONTROL OF YOUR PHYSICAL AND MENTAL HEALTH

Step-By-Step Summary Riches Are Your Birthright

1 CREATE A WEALTHY MINDSET

2 LEARN FROM AND CHANGE YOUR MONEY STORY

3 CONNECT THE WEALTHY MINDSET WITH ABUNDANCE

4 FORGE A PATCH FOR AN ABUNDANT LIFE

WEALTHY MINDSET + ABUNDANCE = UNLIMITED LIFE

THE PATH WITH THE DESTINATION OF AN ABUNDANT LIFE IS BEFORE YOU

7. CONTINUE TO CONQUER AND REPLACE NEGATIVE THOUGHTS AS YOU SHIFT ANY LIMITING BELIEFS TO A MORE ABUNDANT MINDSET

⬇

What negative thoughts will you strive to be rid of in your life?

⬇

What is your reframe of those negative thoughts to convert them into a more positive way of thinking?

> "THE KEY TO ABUNDANCE IS MEETING LIMITED CIRCUMSTANCES WITH UNLIMITED THOUGHTS."
>
> – MARIANNE WILLIAMSON

THE PATH WITH THE HORIZON OF AN ABUNDANT LIFE IN VIEW

4. SURROUND YOURSELF WITH PEOPLE WHO SUPPORT AND ENCOURAGE YOU.

⬇

Identify people you need to spend less time with and where can you seek out more people to support you?

⬇

5. WHAT MANTRA CAN YOU SAY EVERY TIME YOU FEEL STUCK, DISCOURAGED, OR IN A CYCLE OF LIMITING BELIEFS?

⬇

My Mantra is....

6. SEEK OUT BOOKS, PODCASTS, AND RESOURCES THAT INSPIRE AND GROW YOUR KNOWLEDGE.

⬇

What topics do you want to focus on first?

THE PATH CONTINUES

2. FOCUS YOUR ENERGY ON WHAT YOU WANT (NOT WHAT YOU DON'T WANT). WRITE GOALS. MAKE A VISION BOARD. VISUALIZE.

What does this look like? (See Chapter Four in this Book)

3. PRACTICE MINDFULNESS AND GRATITUDE DAILY. THE MORE PRESENT AND GRATEFUL YOU ARE THE MORE YOU WILL ATTRACT.

How will you be more mindful and present? (See Chapter Two)

How will you practice gratitude? (See Chapter Six)

THE PATH FOR AN ABUNDANT LIFE

ACHIEVING OUR GOALS IS DEPENDENT ON WHETHER WE TAKE ACTION. MAP OUT YOUR PATH BELOW TO SHOW YOU THE WAY TO YOUR ABUNDANT LIFE.

1.
2. SET CLEAR AND SPECIFIC GOALS (5 YEARS, 1 YEAR, AND 90-DAY GOALS)

In five years I want....

In one year I want....

90 day goal + action steps

What will these goals give you?

Why are these goals important to you?

WHAT CAN I DO TO CREATE WEALTH?

_____

_____

_____

_____

_____

_____

_____

_____

_____

_____

_____

_____

_____

DEDICATED BRAINWRITING

THE WEALTH AND ABUNDANCE CONNECTION

ADVANCE A WEALTHY MINDSET WITH AN ABUNDANT LIFE

WEALTH AND ABUNDANCE CAN BECOME PART OF YOUR LIFE.

FOCUS.

VISUALIZE,

TAKE ACTION.

CALL THEM INTO YOUR LIFE NOW.

A QUEEN DOESN'T NEED TO STRUGGLE OR FEAR SCARCITY.

HOW WILL YOU DEVELOP YOUR WEALTHY MINDSET?

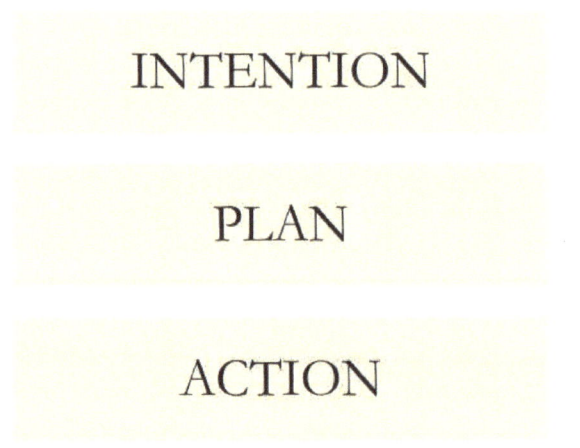

INTENTION

PLAN

ACTION

GENERATIONAL WEALTH

"When money flows into the hands of women, who have the authority to use it, everything changes — for women, their families, and their communities."
- Melinda Gates

While wealthy families plan for three to five generations in advance, those with a scarcity mentality plan for Saturday night. Yet, women are readily empowered and capable of establishing generational wealth, impactful legacies, initiating educational funds for their children, and financial security. Will you be the one to break the familial history of any adverse or habitually poor money habits? The most luxurious life you can lead is one of financial peace and freedom.

YOUR MONEY STORY
PART III

 WHAT DOES MONEY REPRESENT TO YOU (STABILITY, HAPPINESS, STRESS, DISCOMFORT, WORTH)?	
HOW WOULD YOU DESCRIBE YOUR ROLE WITH MONEY? Generous, Spender, Investor, Good Steward, Saver, Miser, Fixer, Philanthropist, Other	
 DID YOUR FAMILY OR SOMEONE CLOSE TO YOU EXPERIENCE A SIGNIFICANT FINANCIAL EVENT AND HOW DID THAT IMPACT YOU?	
DESCRIBE THE EMOTIONS THAT COME UP WITH MONEY AND FINANCIAL MATTERS, IN GENERAL?	
 WHAT HAVE THESE QUESTIONS REVEALED TO YOU ABOUT YOUR RELATIONSHIP WITH MONEY?	

YOUR MONEY STORY
PART II

	DO YOU HAVE GUILT ABOUT MONEY? IF SO WHY?	
	DO YOU THINK YOU DESERVE AN ABUNDANCE OF MONEY? WHY OR WHY NOT?	
	DO YOU CONSIDER YOURSELF FINANCIALLY SUCCESSFUL? WHAT DOES THAT LOOK LIKE?	
	WHAT DEFINES FINANCIAL FREEDOM TO YOU?	
	DID THE CULTURE YOU GREW UP IN IMPACT YOUR RELATIONSHIP WITH MONEY?	

YOUR MONEY STORY

THE PROMPTS BELOW WILL REVEAL YOUR RELATIONSHIP WITH MONEY

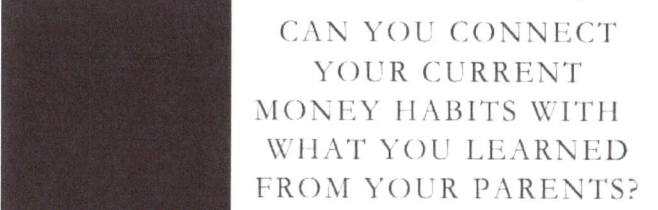

WHAT DOES YOUR LIFE TODAY REVEAL ABOUT WHAT YOU BELIEVE REGARDING MONEY?	
CAN YOU CONNECT YOUR CURRENT MONEY HABITS WITH WHAT YOU LEARNED FROM YOUR PARENTS?	
WHAT STRUGGLES HAVE YOU EXPERIENCED THAT ARE DIRECTLY RELATED TO MONEY?	
WHAT ARE YOU DOING DIFFERENTLY THAN WHAT PARENTS DID WITH MONEY AND WHY?	
GROWING UP, DID YOU HAVE MORE OR LESS THAN YOUR PEERS AND HOW DID THAT AFFECT YOU?	

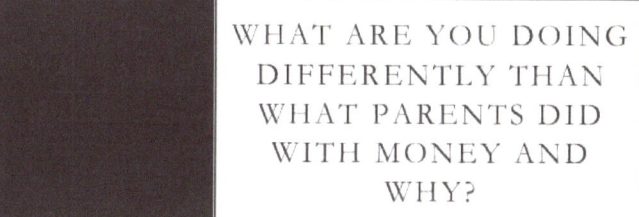

CREATE A WEALTHY MINDSET PART II

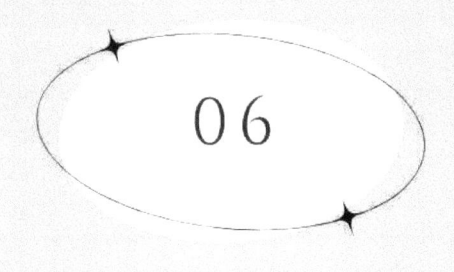

06

INVEST IN HIRED HELP
Be willing to spend money to save time and allow you to do what only you can do. Outsource the tasks you don't like, aren't talented in, or can delegate to allow you to perform your highest purpose.

07

BE PRODUCTIVE-NOT BUSY
Be intentional about how you invest your time. Be clear about the result you want to accomplish before you start.

08

LEARN HIGH PERFORMANCE FOCUS SKILLS
Master high performance focus skills. Become laser-focused and you will achieve more in less time and at your best.

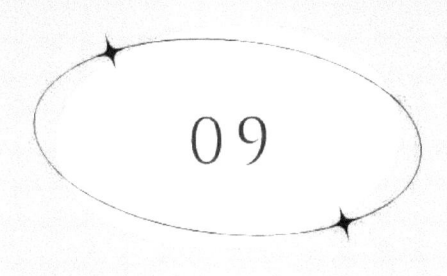

09

MAKE SELF-CARE AND SELF-LOVE A PRIORITY
Honor and value yourself and your needs. Take care of YOU so as to give your best rather than what's left. Take time to relax, renew, and recharge scheduling time for you. Take breaks, personal time, and vacations.

10

VALUE YOUR WORTH
Appreciate your experience, education, skills, and expertise. Don't discount, devalue, or diminish.

CREATE A WEALTHY MINDSET

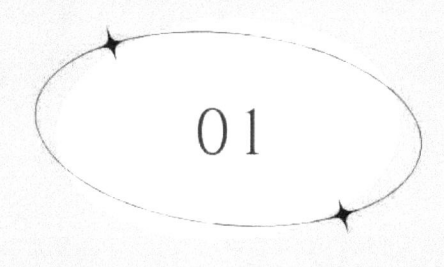

01

LEARN TO ASK FOR WHAT YOU WANT

Don't be afraid to hear NO. Have the confidence to ask for what you want. They may say no, but more often you will hear a YES.

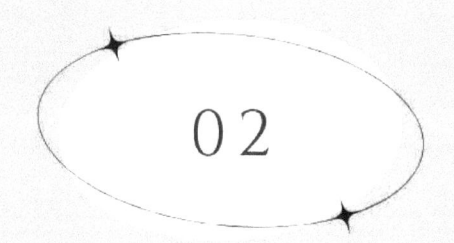

02

LEARN NEW THINGS

Foster a growth mindset. Recognize opportunities. If nothing ever changes, you are not growing.

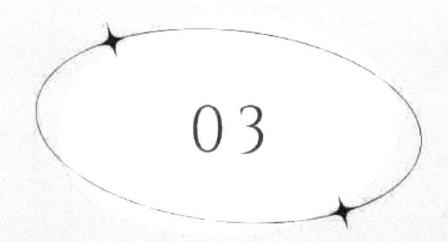

03

VALUE YOUR NETWORK

Social capital can be your most valuable asset. Learn to connect and collaborate. You will go further faster.

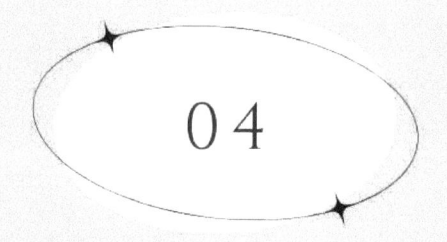

04

REFER AND SUPPORT OTHERS

Become known as someone who will refer the people they trust and supports others. People, in turn, will return the favor.

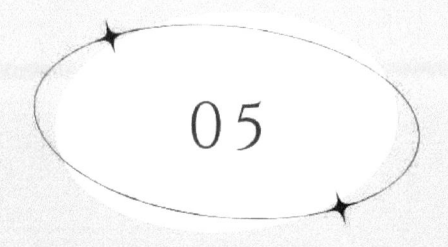

05

SEEK OUT MENTORSHIP

Save time and money by seeking out those who are where you want to be. Find ways to serve them and appreciate and respect their time and efforts.

RICHES ARE YOUR BIRTHRIGHT

CREATE A WEALTHY MINDSET
YOUR MONEY STORY
LIVE AN ABUNDANT LIFE

CHAPTER NINE

Riches Are Your Birthright

A WEALTHY MINDSET · AN ANBUNDANT LIFE

DEVELOP A WEALTHY MINDSET TO ACTIVATE YOUR ABUNDANT LIFE

Step-By-Step Summary
Fortress of Coping

1 ADDRESS CHEMICAL IMBALANCES

2 STRIVE FOR OPTIMUM EMOTIONAL HEALTH

3 RELEASE TOXIC ENERGY

4 STOP THE SPIRALS, USE POSITIVE SELF-SOOTHING

Positive emotional health + better self-soothing choices =
empowerment for a happy and successful life

MAKE BETTER SELF-SOOTHING CHOICES

NEGATIVE SELF-SOOTHING

Avoidiance Gossip   Excessive
Sleep   Under-   Spending
Drug Use   Eating   Gambling
Alcohol   Binging
Smoking

When I start spiraling. or feel negative emotions, I do this to feel better....

POSITIVE SELF-SOOTHING

Exercise   Laughter   Play
Therapy   Creativity Friends
Writing   Volunteer
Hobbies   Self Care
Sports   Dance

A healthier option is....

SPIRAL STOPPERS

SOOTHING SELF-CARE

Create a space to relax
Stretch
Take a warm bath/shower
Relax your body
Focused breathing
Release tension
Seek out soothing imagery
Calming music
Self-compassion

EMERGENCY RELIEF KIT

Essential Oils
Stress Balls
Pen and Journal
Stress-Relief Candles
Dark Chocolate
Affirmation Cards
Herbal Tea
Positive Playlist

STIMULATE THE FIVE SENSES

Five things you see around you
Four things you can touch around you
Three things you hear
Two things you can smell
One thing you can taste

YOUR PERSONAL SPIRAL-STOPPERS

BE PREPARED AND READY
TO STOP A SPIRAL

- HAVE A SELF-CARE SOOTHING PLAN
- STIMULATE THE FIVE SENSES
- HAVE AN EMERGENCY RELIEF KIT

STOP THE SPIRAL

FEELINGS OF LOSS, SUPPRESSED EMOTIONS, SHAME, & GUILT

A spiral is a situation with a series of negative thoughts, emotions, and actions that feeds back into itself, causing the situation to progressively worsen.

Spiral diagram labeled with: NEGATIVE EXPERIENCES, SUPPRESSED EMOTIONS, RUMINATION, PHYSICAL DISTRESS, UNHEALTHY BEHAVIOR

STRATEGY: 1. ENGAGE YOUR EMPOWERMENT; 2. PRACTICE SELF-SOOTHING; AND SHIFT YOUR THOUGHTS

WAYS TO RELEASE TOXIC ENERGY

IN YOUR HOME
Deep-clean your home
Declutter and organize
Create a no-complaining rule
Share gratitude's at dinner time
Pray over your home
Air out the house
Incense/smudging
Add plants
Bring in light
Allow sunshine in
Place crystals around
Candles
Fresh flowers
New paint
Add art
Feng Shui
Play music

WITH YOUR BODY
Reiki
Soak in the Bath
Essential oils
Immerse yourself in nature
Visualize light surrounding you
Be still and relax your body
breathe deeply
Allow your thoughts to untangle and flow
Move your body, shake it out
Smile and laugh
Fuel your body with nutrition
Hydrate with water
practice kindness
Let go and Let God
Forgive and set yourself free
Emotion code sessions

ARE YOU EMOTIONALLY HEALTHY?

GIVE EACH A SCORE OF 1-10 WITH "1" BEING THE LOWEST IN YOUR EMOTIONAL HEALTH AND "10" BEING THE HIGHEST SCORE YOU CAN GIVE YOURSELF

01   I am comfortable with my feelings

02   I am able to express or journal how I feel

03   I talk about feelings

04   I am able to vocalize how I feel

05   I don't judge or condemn my feelings

06   I allow myself to feel my emotions

07   I'm able to express my feelings without guilt or shame

08   I acknowledge and accept my and others' feelings

09   I explore the reasons for my feelings

10   I don't apologize for my emotions

REFLECTION NOTES

Emotional Health

TRAPPED EMOTIONS

Trapped emotions that have been stuffed in order to survive get in the way. They sabotage our efforts to create the life we want and make us miserable. Freeing this emotional energy stuck in our bodies is exactly what we need to feel free and fully live so we can experience our best life. It's time to face and feel the emotional feelings you've been avoiding. Emotional baggage is real not just an expression. When you feel stress, trauma, or distress, your body remembers even if your mind forgets or blocks out the past.

It's s a survival mechanism that your brain and body are programmed to assist you. But when not brought back to a neutral state and released, that same emotional baggage can wreak havoc on your mind and body in the form of muscle tension, limiting beliefs, and negative emotional triggers.

All of these are toxic to your body, as well as, the energy they create. The burden of carrying this "emotional baggage" and toxic energy can derail you from the life you desire and keep you from your true power and purpose.

WAYS TO INCREASE THESE CHEMICALS NATURALLY

- Probiotics - Fish Oil- Omega 3 - Green Tea - Magnesium - Ginkgo & Ginseng - Caffeine - Vitamin D/Sun - Cold Showers - Deep Breathing - Singing - Exercise - Intermittent Fasting - Limit Sugar - Stand More - Theanine Supplement - Less Gluten - Less Dairy	- Hugging (try heart to heart for 8 seconds) - Kissing - Cuddling - Sexual Intimacy & Orgasm - Massage & Physical Touch - Social Interaction - Pet an Animal - Dance - Yoga - Meditation - Vitamin D - Magnesium - Self-Care Practices - AM/PM Rituals - Regular and Balanced Meals - Eat in the company of others - Avoid Caffeine	- Eat more turkey and salmon - Aerobic Exercise - Sunlight - Time in Nature - Pure Tryptophan - Probiotics - St. John's Wort - Massage Therapy - Visualization - 8 Hours + Sleep - Laugh & Play - Socialize - Help Others - Therapy	- Exercise - Laugh - Music - Acupuncture - Dark Chocolate - Sex - Dance - Meditate - Spicy Foods - Rhodiola - Ginseng - Vanilla Bean - Volunteer - Create Art

***The above are tips and not medical advice.

CHEMICAL IMBALANCE
HOW YOU FEEL COULD BE A CHEMICAL IMBALANCE

DOPAMINE

No Motivation
Fatigue
Moody or Anxious
Emotionally Flat
Depressed
Low sex drive
Trouble Sleeping
Brain Fog
Social Anxiety

OXYTOCIN & CORTISOL*

Stressed
Tired
Low Energy
Lonely
Disconnected
Anti-Social
Lack Connection

*These two hormones need to balance each other

SEROTONIN

Moodiness
Anxiety
Sleep issues
Digestive problems
Carbohydrates and Sweets Cravings
Suicidal Ideations
Obsessive Compulsive Disorder (OCD)
Panic Attacks
Rumination of Past

ENDORPHINS

Unintentional Weight Loss
Body Aches and Pains
Depression
Anxiety
Moodiness
Sleep issues
Addiction
Chronic Pain

FORTRESS OF COPING

SELF-SOOTHING TECHNIQUES

CHEMICAL IMBALANCE

EMOTIONAL HEALTH

CHAPTER EIGHT

Fortress of Coping

SELF-SOOTHING

EMOTIONAL HEALTH

POSITIVE SELF-SOOTHING TECHNIQUES AND OVERCOMING ADDICTIVE HABITS

Step-By-Step Summary
Reign Yourself

1 Adopt an open and abundant mindset

2 Conquer limiting beliefs

3 Master your emotions

4 Stay empowered and in control

An abundant mindset + self control + empowerment =
A results-oriented and changed life

EMPOWER YOURSELF!

STAY EMPOWERED

- Practice Self-Care Daily
- Schedule and Manage Your Time
- Establish Boundaries and Say "NO"
- Exercise Regularly
- Eat Nutritious Food
- Get Eight Hours of Sleep
- Limit Your Alcohol Intake
- Stay in Touch with Yourself
- Journal
- Mirror Work

DEVISE A PLAN.
DISEMPOWERED WOMEN LACK SELF-CONTROL.

Circle one area above that you will commit to doing more of to stay empowered. Start today.

EMPOWER

WHAT MAKES YOU FEEL DISEMPOWERED AND VULNERABLE TO TRIGGERS?

Check all that apply.

- [ ] Over-scheduling my calendar
- [ ] Not enough "ME" time
- [ ] Absence of healthy boundaries
- [ ] Over-working, too many hours, and extrem intensity
- [ ] Tolerating things that make me unhappy
- [ ] Being out of touch with myself
- [ ] Drinking, eating, or other addictive behaviors
- [ ] Disempowering habits (TV, scrolling on social media)
- [ ] Relationships
- [ ] Insecurity
- [ ] Financial Problems
- [ ] Stress
- [ ] Illness
- [ ] Emotional/Physical Pain
- [ ] Sleep Deprivation
- [ ] Hunger
- [ ] Lack of Confidence

WHAT DISEMPOWERS YOU?

Identifying triggers explains our reactions but it doesn't excuse them. You are responsible for your reactions and how you choose to react directly impacts your life.

If you really want life to change, it begins with controlling your reactions.

But when you have a moment to yourself, be kind to you. You are human and self-condemnation only makes it worse. Identify your triggers and practice a different response than what you've previously and habitually had. In time, you will learn how to control your reactions faster. You will master your emotions and command your habits.

SELF-CONTROL

Like a city whose walls are broken through is a person who lacks self-control

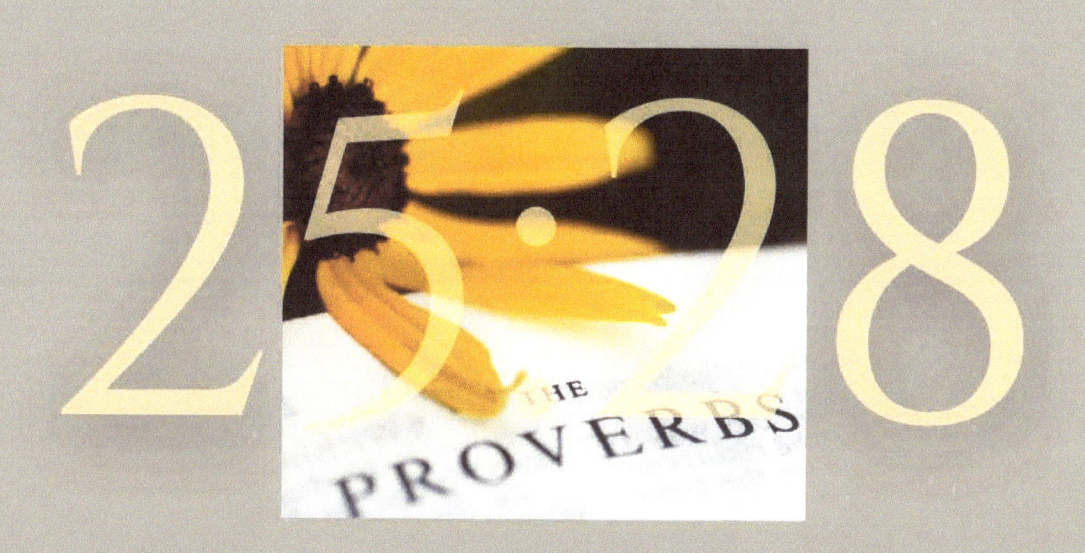

25:28 PROVERBS

Why is it that something that makes you totally lose it...doesn't upset someone else?
- Different values or personality
- Belief system about how things *should be*
- Perceptions based on esteem experience

OVERCOMING A LIMITING MINDSET

QUESTIONS TO CHALLENGE YOUR NEGATIVE MINDSET

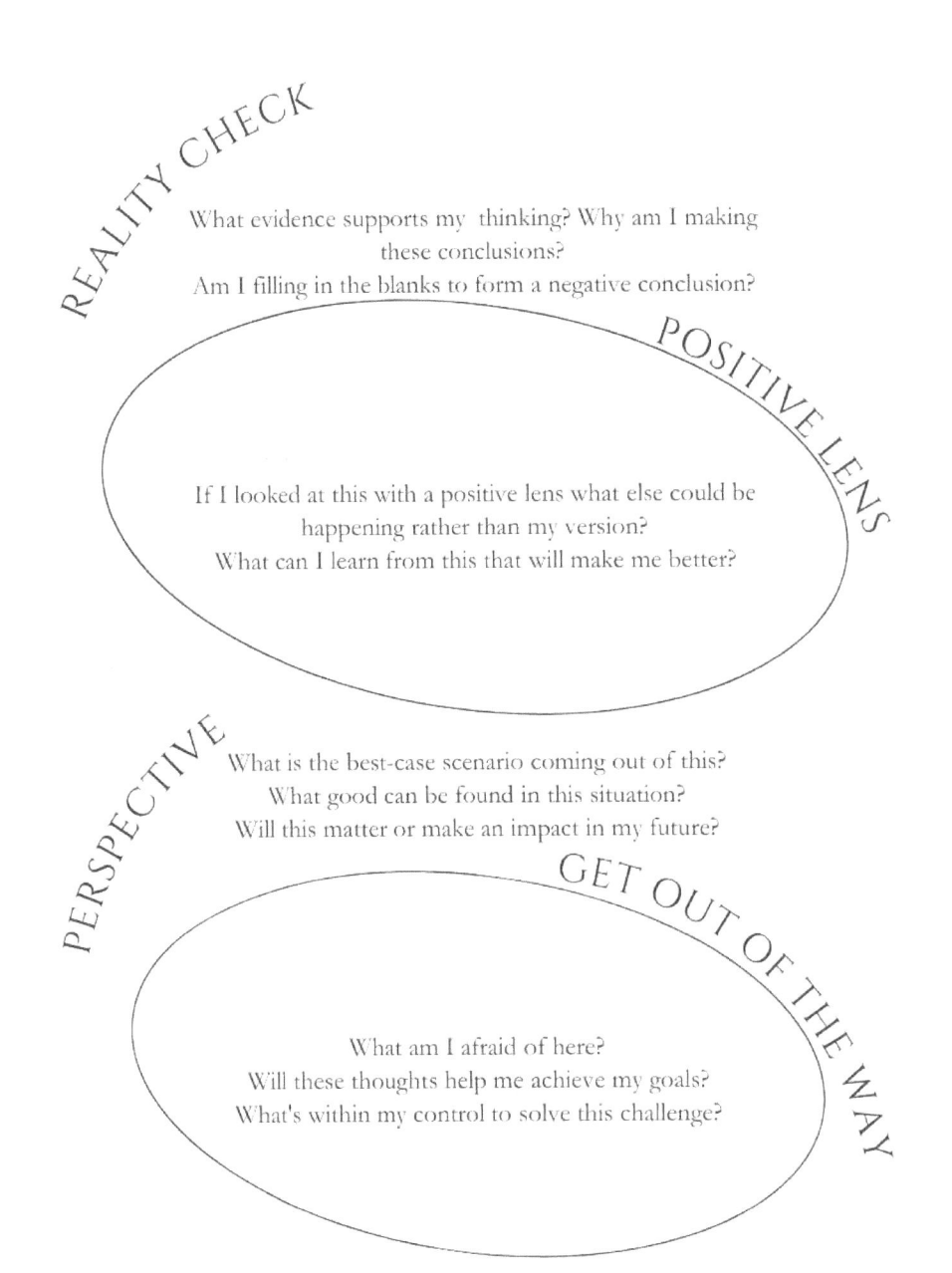

REALITY CHECK

What evidence supports my thinking? Why am I making these conclusions?
Am I filling in the blanks to form a negative conclusion?

POSITIVE LENS

If I looked at this with a positive lens what else could be happening rather than my version?
What can I learn from this that will make me better?

PERSPECTIVE

What is the best-case scenario coming out of this?
What good can be found in this situation?
Will this matter or make an impact in my future?

GET OUT OF THE WAY

What am I afraid of here?
Will these thoughts help me achieve my goals?
What's within my control to solve this challenge?

MASTER YOUR EMOTIONS
ANALYZE YOUR TRIGGERS

An emotional trigger can draw you into your past. One can be reminded of pain and suffering from childhood or past experiences which then causes old feelings and behaviors to arise.
It can, however, cause a person to launch into habitual or addictive ways of trying to manage those difficult feelings.

Because your response is habitual it can be challenging to identify the exact trigger unless you take the time to analyze what is going on in and around you. The best way to gain self-control is to identify where the root of the trigger lies. You can then heal that part of yourself and replace the old triggers with new perspectives and new behaviors.

Identify the cause of the trigger by analyzing the internal and external evidence. The internal involves thoughts, feelings, and perceptions. The external includes situations, social environment, and people. Ask yourself, "Where is this coming from?"

Choose a situation that triggers you and sends you into a downward spiral. Try to identify the root. When is the earliest memory of this bothering you? Typical triggers can include rejection, disapproval, shame, criticism, neediness, abandonment, helplessness, controlled, or being left out. With this process, you will begin to master your emotions.

DEVELOPING AN ABUNDANT MINDSET

- Do/Experience something different on a regular basis
- Practice gratitude (it happens for you not to you)
- Complete whatever you decide to start no matter how hard it is
- Make a physical change; redecorate; get a makeover; change up your routine
- Set healthy boundaries for yourself and others

1. What is something new you can learn or experience?

2. What do you need to complete? How will finishing it benefit your life?

3. Where can you make a physical change?

4. Where do you need to set a stronger boundary?

5. What area of your life do you need to have more gratitude?

- Corral negative thoughts and replace them with positive mantras
- Make a commitment to stay empowered in life without using substances
- Do something you've never done
- Practice generosity: Give more than you think you can and be a servant to others
- Be present and feel content and satisfied during even the simplest things

MINDSET CHECKLIST

ACKNOWLEDGE WHERE YOU HAVE AN ABUNDANT MINDSET

17	I FAIL A LOT BECAUSE I TRY NEW THINGS	YES ☐	NO ☐
18	I STRIVE AT LIVING LIFE TO THE FULLEST	YES ☐	NO ☐
	TOTAL NUMBER OF "YES"	YES ☐	
	TOTAL NUMBER OF "NO"		NO ☐

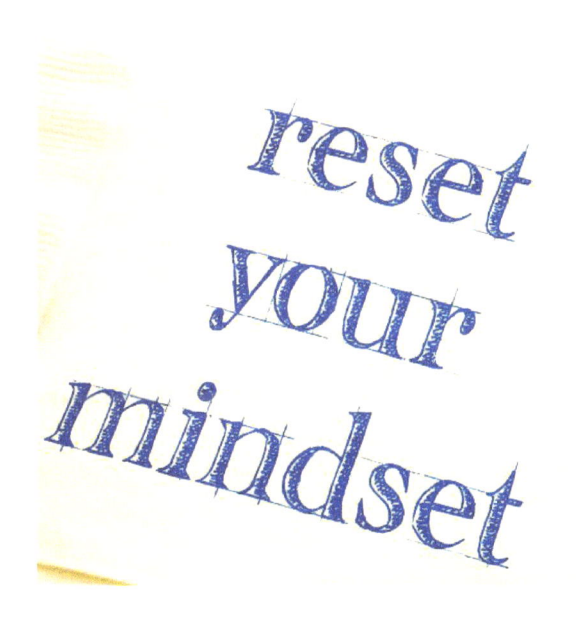

reset your mindset

MINDSET CHECKLIST

ACKNOWLEDGE WHERE YOU HAVE AN *ABUNDANT* MINDSET

09	I'M WILLING TO BE VULNERABLE	YES ☐	NO ☐
10	I DON'T LET FEAR STOP ME FROM DOING THINGS	YES ☐	NO ☐
11	I RARELY FEEL LIMITED	YES ☐	NO ☐
12	I CAN PRETTY MUCH DO ANYTHING I SET MY MIND TO ACHIEVE	YES ☐	NO ☐
13	I DON'T LET OTHERS CONTROL MY HAPPINESS	YES ☐	NO ☐
14	I AM RARELY ANXIOUS	YES ☐	NO ☐
15	I'M WILLING TO BE UNCOMFORTABLE	YES ☐	NO ☐
16	I'M TYPICALLY A HAPPY PERSON	YES ☐	NO ☐

MINDSET CHECKLIST

*ACKNOWLEDGE WHERE YOU HAVE AN **ABUNDANT** MINDSET*

01	I LIKE TO FIGURE THINGS OUT	YES ☐	NO ☐
02	I LIKE LEARNING NEW THINGS	YES ☐	NO ☐
03	I CAN BE FLEXIBLE	YES ☐	NO ☐
04	I'M WILLING TO STEP OUT OF MY AREAS OF KNOWLEDGE	YES ☐	NO ☐
05	I BELIEVE MISTAKES MAKE ME BETTER	YES ☐	NO ☐
06	I'M ABLE TO PUSH MYSELF THROUGH CHALLENGES	YES ☐	NO ☐
07	I'M AN OVERCOMER	YES ☐	NO ☐
08	I INVEST EFFORT INTO MAKING MY DREAMS COME TRUE	YES ☐	NO ☐

CHANGE YOUR MINDSET

CHANGE YOUR LIFE

MINDSET CHECKLIST

ACKNOWLEDGE WHERE YOU HAVE A *FIXED* MINDSET

		YES	NO
17	LIFE FEELS HARD	☐	☐
18	I DON'T LIKE LEARNING	☐	☐
	TOTAL NUMBER OF "YES"	☐	
	TOTAL NUMBER OF "NO"		☐

MINDSET CHECKLIST

ACKNOWLEDGE WHERE YOU HAVE A FIXED MINDSET

09   I DON'T LIKE CHANGE   YES ☐   NO ☐

10   I PREFER THINGS TO STAY THE SAME   YES ☐   NO ☐

11   I DON'T HAVE OPPORTUNITIES   YES ☐   NO ☐

12   PEOPLE IRRITATE ME   YES ☐   NO ☐

13   I HAVE A LOT OF ANXIETY   YES ☐   NO ☐

14   FEAR HOLDS ME BACK   YES ☐   NO ☐

15   I'M MOSTLY UNHAPPY   YES ☐   NO ☐

16   I RARELY FAIL   YES ☐   NO ☐

MINDSET CHECKLIST

ACKNOWLEDGE WHERE YOU HAVE A FIXED MINDSET

		YES	NO
01	I AVOID ANYTHING CHALLENGING	☐	☐
02	I HAVE FEW NEW EXPERIENCES	☐	☐
03	I OFTEN QUIT WHEN IT GETS DIFFICULT	☐	☐
04	I GET FRUSTRATED WITH SETBACKS	☐	☐
05	I'M EASILY ANGERED	☐	☐
06	I FEEL STUCK	☐	☐
07	I DON'T HAVE CHOICES	☐	☐
08	I SAY "I CAN'T" A LOT	☐	☐

REIGN YOURSELF

SELF CONTROL
MASTER YOUR EMOTIONS
COMMAND YOUR HABITS
DEVELOP AN ABUNDANT MINDSET

CHANGE YOUR MINDSET CHANGE YOUR LIFE

A MINDSET is a collection of beliefs, ideas, and attitudes that shape the way someone thinks about themselves and the world. Your mindset will determine how you behave, your outlook, and your attitudes towards life and people. A mindset can either cause you to spot an opportunity or trap you in a self-sabotaging cycle, as well as, determining whether you are able to create success or will live in constant struggle.

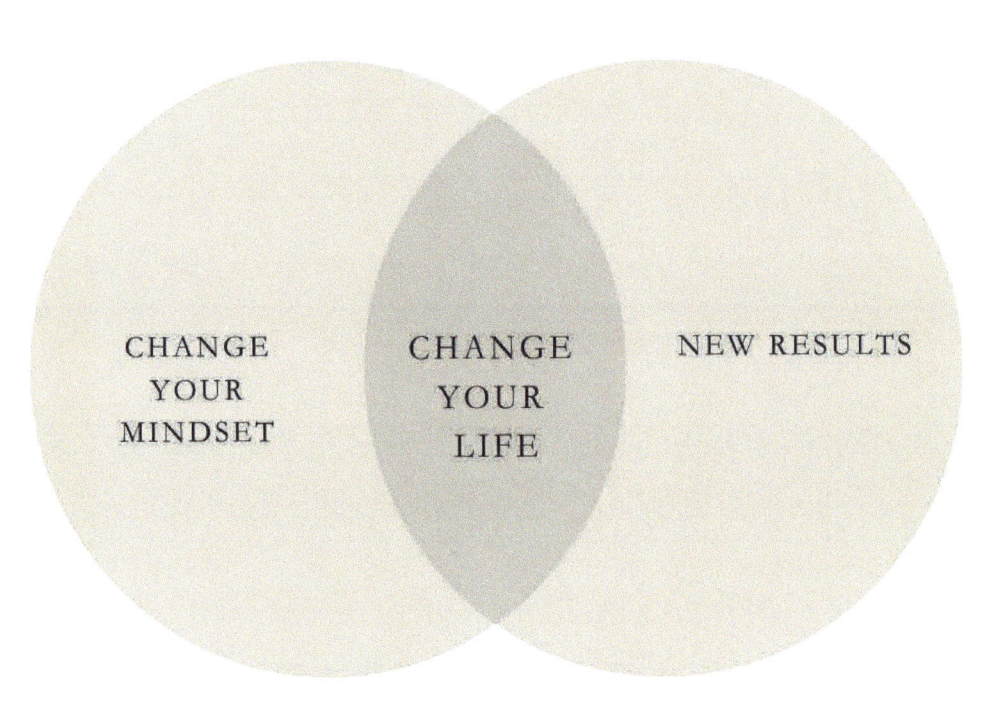

CHANGE YOUR MINDSET | CHANGE YOUR LIFE | NEW RESULTS

HOW TO CHANGE
A MINDSET

1. Identify where you have a FIXED MINDSET
2. Recognize the choices you need to create for change
3. Plan an attack on your fixed mindset
4. Take action on your plan
5. Talk to your inner critic
6. Give yourself grace and encouragement
7. Practice, practice, practice

CHAPTER SEVEN

Reign Yourself

SELF-CONTROL

MASTER YOUR EMOTIONS

CREATE HABITS FOR A RESULTS-ORIENTED LIFE

STEP-BY-STEP SUMMARY SEIZE YOUR SHIELD OF SATISFACTION

1 EMPOWER YOURSELF

2 TRAIN CONSISTENTLY FOR THE MIND-BODY CONNECTION OF HAPPINESS

3 LIVE YOUR PASSION

4 PRACTICE GRATITUDE DAILY

HAPPINESS + PASSION + GRATITUDE = AN EMPOWERED AND SATISFYING LIFE

Daily Gratitude

Gratitude will promote you seeing your life and the world in a more positive light. It will also empower you to press through some of life's most difficult challenges.

Daily Gratitude

PRACTICE GRATITUDE

Make a list of as many items as you can in gratitude.
Make it a daily/nightly habit and watch your life change.

Gratitude Jou

WAYS TO PRACTICE GRATITUDE
- *Appreciate everything*
- *Seek the good in all circumstances*
- *Be mindful and appreciate the moment*
- *Say three things you are grateful for each morning upon rising and/or going to bed*
- *Give generously*
- *Praise and compliment often*
- *Always show appreciation to those who serve you*

Your environment to thrive

01 Physical surroundings

02 Mental stimulation

03 The people around you

04 Distractors to dispose, declutter, donate, or diffuse

Design a setting for happiness

Stay Empowered: Live Your Passions

A secret component to a fulfilled life lies in your passions

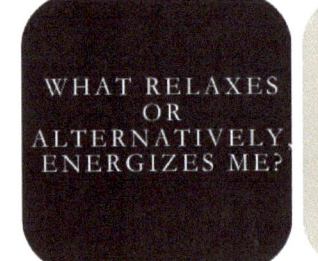

- WHAT RELAXES OR ALTERNATIVELY, ENERGIZES ME?
- WHAT DID I DREAM OF DOING BEFORE I WAS TOLD WHO I AM?
- IF MONEY WASN'T A CONSIDERATION, WHAT WOULD I BE DOING?
- WHAT IS MY CALLING? WHAT SPEAKS TO MY HEART? WHAT IS MY DESTINY OR PURPOSE ON EARTH?

My Passions

WHAT LIGHTS YOU UP?

Happiness is an Inside Job
The Mind-Body Connection

1/
POSITIVITY BEGETS SUCCESS

Positive brains have a biological advantage over neutral or negative brains. Retrain and rewire your brain to be positive, happy, and successful.

2/
CHOOSE HAPPINESS

Choose to be happy (Have faith that all will work out for the good).

Do whatever it takes (Don't give up when it gets uncomfortable or hard).

Accept you are worthy of the life you desire and to be happy.

3/
ACCEPT THAT ONLY YOU HAVE THE KEYS TO YOUR HAPPINESS

Stop waiting on others or on life's events to make you feel happy. Only YOU have that POWER.

4/
INCORPORATE BRAIN BOOSTERS IN YOUR LIFE

Keep your mind sharp and healthy. Allow the successful creation of new neural pathways for happiness to continue developing throughout your life. Happiness occurs when the mind and body connect.

How to be Happier Today

ALL FEELINGS start with your thoughts. When you experience heaviness, sadness, anxiety, depression or even a bad mood, it's time to deal with the negativity playing havoc in your brain. Tune into that "radio station" in your head and become the director of your thoughts. Consistent training will stop the dwelling on the perceived negative consequences and alleviate those unhappy feelings.

Instant Mood Changers

- Sunshine
- Meditation
- Nap
- Deep Breathing
- Laughter
- Upbeat Music
- Change of Scenery
- Human Contact
- Organize
- Clean
- Take a Bath/Shower
- Engage in a Passion
- Play
- Hug
- Express your Creativity
- Affirmations
- Journal/Write
- Wear something that makes you feel good
- Give yourself a facial
- Wander in a Bookstore

HAPPINESS ASSESSMENT

How happy are you (really) in each of these areas?

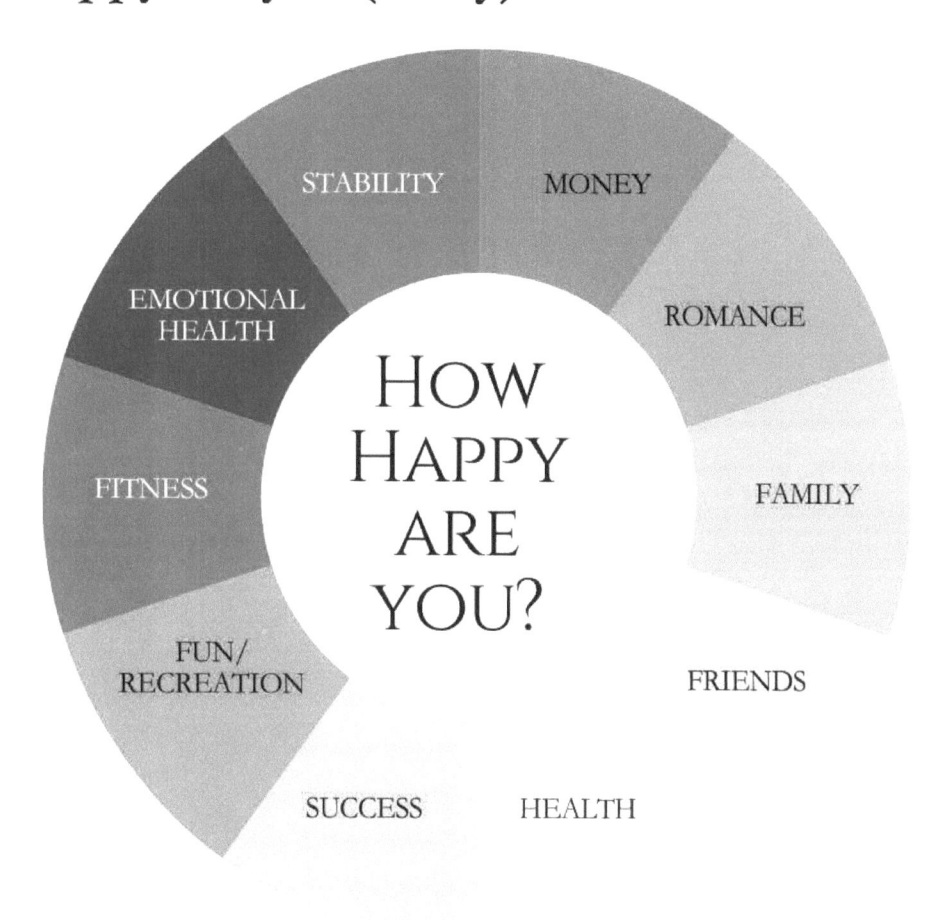

Wheel categories: STABILITY, MONEY, ROMANCE, FAMILY, FRIENDS, HEALTH, SUCCESS, FUN/RECREATION, FITNESS, EMOTIONAL HEALTH — HOW HAPPY ARE YOU?

01 Rate each area of your life

1. Miserable
2. Mostly unhappy
3. I'm struggling
4. I tolerate it
5. Meh (don't think about it)
6. Trying to be happy
7. Making progress
8. Content with it
9. Pretty happy
10. Very Happy!

02 For the lowest scored areas, what would happiness look like?

SEIZE THE SHIELD OF SATISFACTION

BECOME AN EMPOWERED YOU

THE HAPPINESS MIND CONNECTION

LIVE YOUR PASSION

THE GIFT OF GRATITUDE

CHAPTER SIX
Seize the Shield of Satisfaction

EMPOWERING YOURSELF

HAPPINESS AND GRATITUDE

LEARN THE SECRETS TO AN EMPOWERED, HAPPY, AND SATISFYING LIFE

Step-By-Step Summary Proclaim Grace

1 FORGIVE YOURSELF

2 EXTEND GRACE

3 BE KIND AND GENTLE TO YOURSELF

4 RELEASE JUDGMENT

Forgiveness + grace + Self-Kindness + release of judgment =
Overcoming yourself and experience breakthroughs to the next level

Forgiveness is a gift to yourself. It frees you from the past, past experiences, and past relationships. It allows you to live in the present time. When you forgive yourself and forgive others, you are indeed free.

—Louise Hay

LET GO OF JUDGMENT OF OTHERS

Next time you catch yourself judging another person, ask yourself these questions:

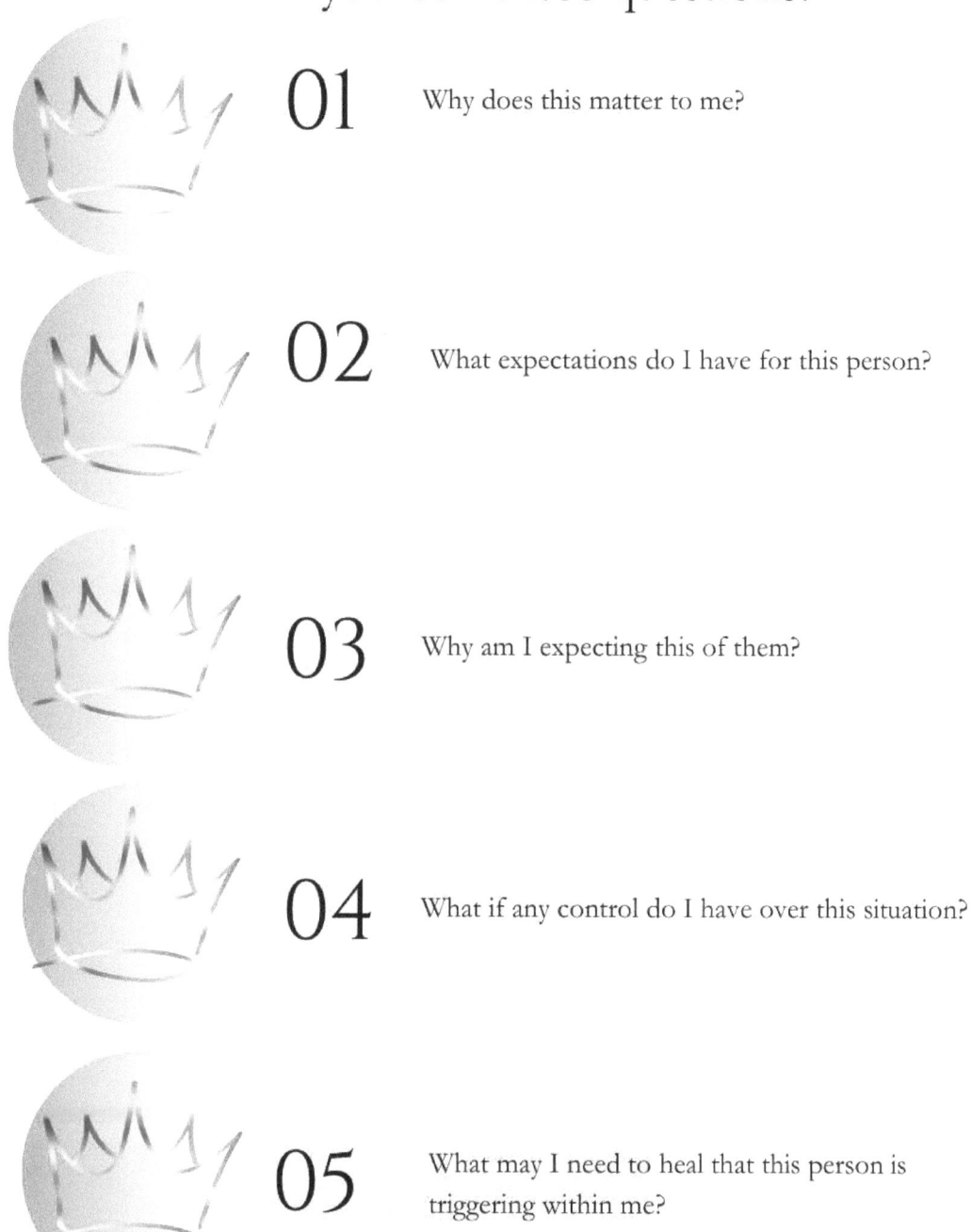

01 Why does this matter to me?

02 What expectations do I have for this person?

03 Why am I expecting this of them?

04 What if any control do I have over this situation?

05 What may I need to heal that this person is triggering within me?

HOW WILL YOU EXTEND GRACE TO YOURSELF?

BE KIND AND GENTLE WITH YOURSELF

Extend grace

Give yourself grace when you make mistakes.
Failures are our best lessons. Don't let mistakes create shame and guilt. Remind yourself you are human and try to avoid making the same mistake again.

Stop expecting perfection from yourself.
It is healthy to strive for excellence but perfection is born out of ego and fear of judgment. Focus on the process not perfection.

When you feel stress from making a mistake, take a break and breathe. Breathing calms your nervous system and helps you to release stress, shame, and guilt. Those negative emotions have zero benefits. Don't beat yourself up by ruminating. Let it go!

Give yourself the grace to feel uncomfortable.
Embrace change and new experiences to get out of your comfort zone. It is said that the treasure you seek is within the cave you fear to enter. Be brave and explore.

Be patient with yourself and give yourself time to make positive changes. You sometimes expect to change overnight but that's not always possible. Long-lasting change takes time and consistency. Give yourself unconditional love and empathy when you are facing the discomforts of personal growth or healing.

Forgive Yourself

"What I learned to do many years ago was to forgive myself. It is very important for every human being to forgive herself or himself because if you live, you will make mistakes - it is inevitable.

But once you do and you see the mistake, then you forgive yourself and say, 'Well, if I'd known better I'd have done better,' that's all. So you say to people who you think you may have injured, 'I'm sorry,' and then you say to yourself, 'I'm sorry.'

If we all hold on to the mistake, we can't see our own glory in the mirror because we have the mistake between our faces and the mirror; we can't see what we're capable of being. You can ask forgiveness of others, but in the end the real forgiveness is in one's own self."

-MAYA ANGELOU

LETTER
to Myself

The "Face It" Strategy

Write a compassionate forgiveness letter to yourself using the "Face It" strategy. Include statements similar to:

I will face....

I forgive myself for hiding and avoiding....

I accept responsibility for....

I commit to doing...to move forward!

I forgive and love myself in spite of....

I've made excuses for...but I forgive myself and take back my power to....

I am sorry for....

I forgive for not trusting myself when....

I will do better by doing....

I learned that....

I let go and release...and give myself the gift of forgiveness.

Forgive yourself

FACE THE ISSUE and refuse to take a victim stance. You can't control the past but you have the power to control what you will do, think, and say going forward.

ACCEPT RESPONSIBILITY and forgive yourself for any part you played in **the issue.**

COMMIT TO MOVE FORWARD by taking positive action instead of staying stuck and feeling sorry for yourself. Self-pity is your enemy. Step beyond the circumstance.

EXCUSES KEEP YOU POWERLESS. It is hard to take responsibility for the consequences of our actions but if you hide your mistakes behind a veil of excuses you will not learn what you need to know in order to become the queen you desire to be.

I'M SORRY are the two most powerful words to eliminate the torture of guilt and shame. Work at making your errors right with yourself and others. Humble yourself.

TRUST YOURSELF. You are capable of doing hard things and overcoming bad habits. Take small steps forward and give yourself grace when you fail. Face it and keep growing.

> "
> **SHINE LIGHT ON YOUR MISTAKES AND THE DARKNESS WILL FLEE!**

PROCLAIM GRACE

OVERCOME YOURSELF
FORGIVE YOURSELF
GIVE YOURSELF GRACE
RELEASE JUDGMENT

CHAPTER FIVE

Proclaim Grace

OVERCOME YOURSELF

FORGIVENESS OF SELF

OVERCOME YOURSELF AND BREAKTHROUGH TO YOUR NEXT LEVEL OF GREATNESS

STEP BY STEP SUMMARY
ACCEPT YOUR TITLE

1 ACKNOWLEDGE AND SHIFT YOUR SELF-IDENTITY

2 DEVELOP AN UNSTOPPABLE CONFIDENCE

3 EVOLVE YOUR NEW AND POSITIVE IDENTITY

4 USE VISUALIZATION AS A CATALYST TO ACTION

AN EVOLVED SELF-IDENTITY +
UNSTOPPABLE CONFIDENCE +
CATALYTIC VISUALIZATION =
A DIRECTED AND SUCCESSFUL LIFE

VISUALIZATION

FOR EMPOWERMENT

Why visualization works

Visualization is a habit successful people have in common. Your mind doesn't know the difference between what is imagined and what is reality. When you visualize your desired outcome you begin to see the possibility of achieving it, reducing resistance and allowing you to take action that will move you toward your dreams.

Try it, it truly works!

Envision Yourself:
Having an achievement
Experiencing a physical object or place
Arriving at a destination or a new level in your business, education, or relationship
Overcoming an obstacle that has kept you from moving forward
Experiencing yourself being the person you want to be

How to visualize to achieve results faster

- First thing in the morning or thirty minutes before bed
- Lay down or in a relaxed position
- Take deep breaths to start
- Let go of tension in every part of your body
- Have your thoughts unwind and swirl freely
- Focus on projecting yourself as someone who has achieved the goal
- Experience how it would feel emotionally to realize the achievement
- Create the sensory specifics in detail around the achievement
- See what is physically different from your current reality
- Imagine how you are different as a person now with what you've achieved
- Picture how you impact those around you after this achievement

**VISUALIZATION DOESN'T REPLACE ACTION.
IT'S A CATALYST TO ACTION.**

Visualization Journal Notes

HOW I FELT AFTER THE VISUALIZATION

POSITIVE AFFIRMATIONS

WHAT I LEARNED OR DISCOVERED FROM THE VISUALIZATION

ACTION STEPS TO BRING THE VISUALIZATION INTO THE PHYSICAL WORLD

MORE OF THIS:

LESS OF THIS:

MY FAVORITE ASPECT OF THE VISUALIZATION

TOMORROW I TAKE ACTION ON MY VISUALIZATION

UNSTOPPABLE

Keep your vision focused.
—Imagine it. See it in technicolor detail.—
Direct your unconscious mind to lead you to a relaxed state of flow.
With calm, clarity, and confidence, access the very best of you and your life.

CONFIDENCE

ALTER EGO EFFECT

Becoming Your Alter Ego (Aspirational Identity)

1. Visualize yourself living your best life.
2. Power Pose (Listen to the TED Talk by Amy Cuddy).
3. Use Affirmations to reprogram with statements you believe.
4. Make a physical change that fosters you feeling like the future you.
5. Take actions that align you with who you want to be.
6. Know how the best thinks, feels, behaves, and lives.
7. Create positive triggers that facilitate you becoming who you desire to be.

WHAT WOULD A DAY IN YOUR
NEW IDENTITY BE LIKE?

Self-Identity Assessment

What changes do you need to make at a Self-Identity level?

01 What negative things do you fear people think about you?

02 What negative things do you think and say about yourself?

03 What parts of yourself do you wish you could change?

Your Self-Identity Is Who You Believe You Are

SELF-IDENTITY & VISION

Long-lasting change happens when you have a shift at the Self-Identity level

Self-Image: How you think others see you
Self-Esteem: How you feel about yourself
Self-Confidence and Self-Acceptance are the Optimum

ACCEPT YOUR TITLE

You are who You Believe You Are

Visualization with Action
Unstoppable Confidence
Step into a New Identity

CHAPTER FOUR

Accept Your Title

SELF-IDENTITY

BECOME YOUR ALTER-EGO

UNDERSTAND HOW YOUR SELF-IDENTITY IS DIRECTING YOUR LIFE

Step By Step Summary
Love the Woman in the Mirror

1 SELF-LOVE WITH YOUR THOUGHTS AND WORDS

2 CLEAR LIMITING BELIEFS THAT ARE HOLDING YOU BACK

3 NO COMPARISON

4 PRACTICE MIRROR WORK AND AFFIRMATIONS

Change your thoughts + Recognize your uniqueness =
A Love of self that is life-changing

No one compares to you!

Comparison and Jealousy can reveal the areas of our lives where we aren't honoring our values and desires. Notice where this is coming up. You will then have insight into where you should focus on improving or letting go.

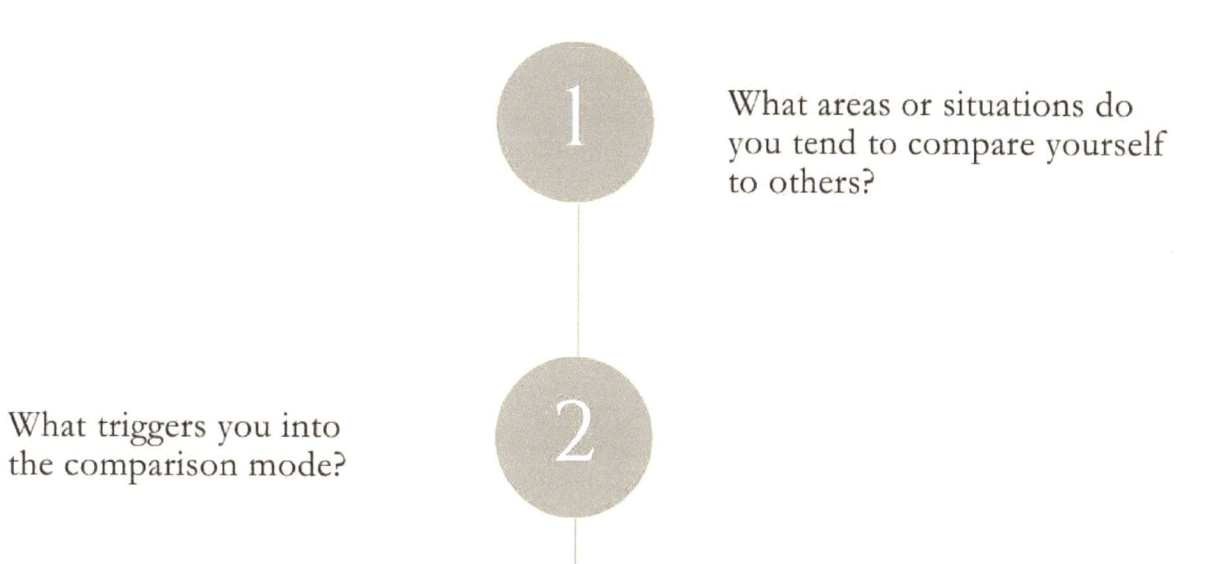

1 — What areas or situations do you tend to compare yourself to others?

2 — What triggers you into the comparison mode?

3 — What do you wish you could change that you have no control over?

4 — What makes you feel "less than" which YOU can change?

Mirror Affirmations List

List ten "I am..." statements to say to yourself

-
-
-
-
-
-
-
-
-
-

MIRROR WORK

Gaze at yourself for 5-10 minutes daily while saying "I am..." affirmations.

Tell yourself something kind every time you look in the mirror

Mirror Work:
- Overcomes your inner critic
- Heals your inner child
- Reprograms your limiting beliefs
- Increases self-love and acceptance
- Improves confidence and self-assuredness

What is Holding You Back?

Identify what is keeping you struggling or feeling unworthy **Part II**

Pride

Independence; Lack of Trust; Ego Wants the Credit

Performance

Earning your worth; Doing it for the applause or validation;
Self-Serving vs. Servant

Problems

Distracted; No Self-Control; Stuck; Apathy

What is Holding You Back?

Identify what is keeping you struggling or feeling unworthy

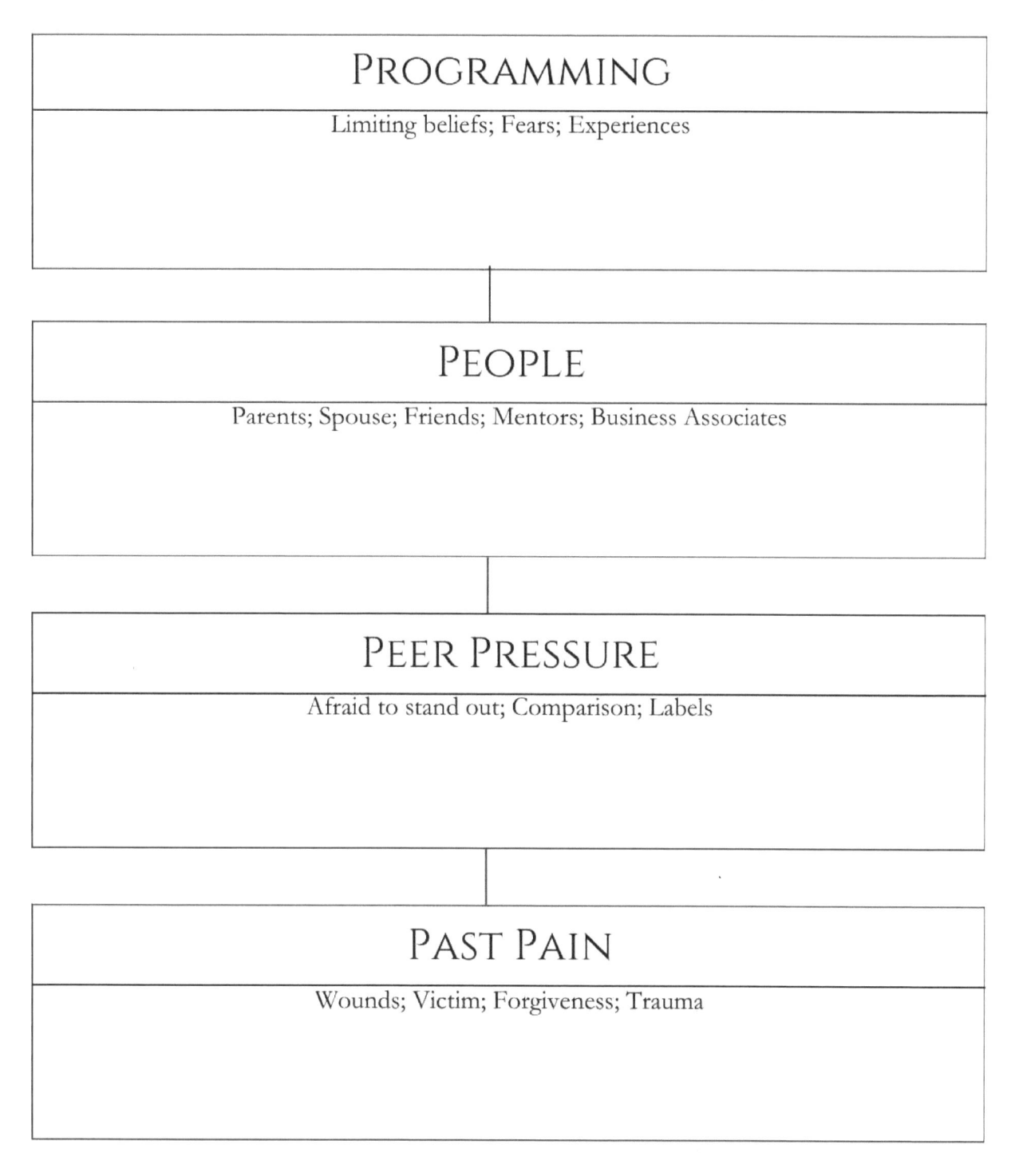

Programming
Limiting beliefs; Fears; Experiences

People
Parents; Spouse; Friends; Mentors; Business Associates

Peer Pressure
Afraid to stand out; Comparison; Labels

Past Pain
Wounds; Victim; Forgiveness; Trauma

IDENTIFYING YOUR LIMITING BELIEFS

What you think is what you say. What you say is what you believe. What you believe is the result you will have!
Your reality reveals the limitations of your beliefs and programming.

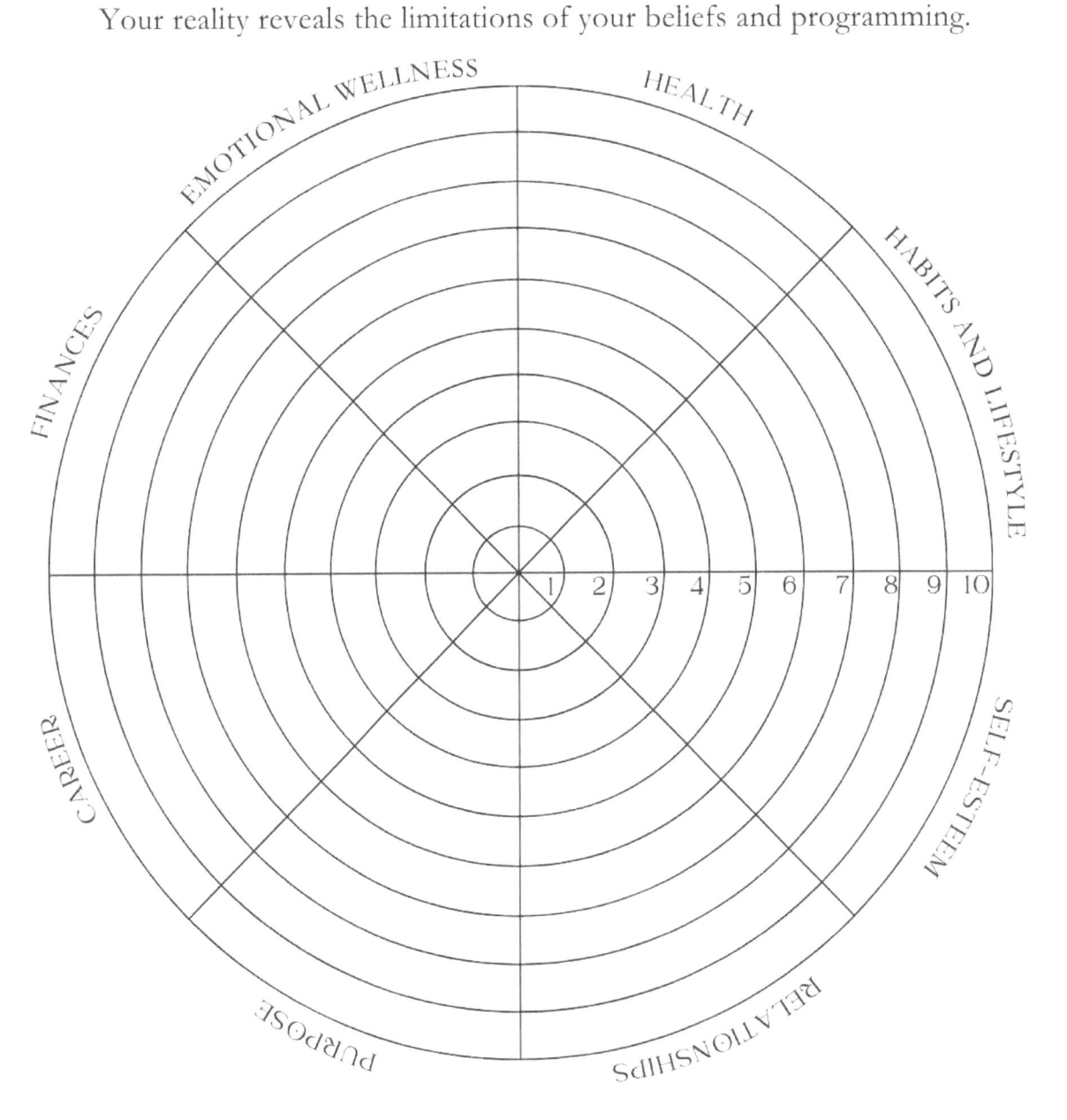

Wheel chart with sections: EMOTIONAL WELLNESS, HEALTH, HABITS AND LIFESTYLE, SELF-ESTEEM, RELATIONSHIPS, PURPOSE, CAREER, FINANCES. Scale 1-10.

1-I need to change~ 2-It's pretty bad~ 3-I'm struggling~ 4-I know but I don't care~ 5-It's average~
6-I make some effort~ 7-I'm working on this~ 8-I'm doing good~ 9-I'm focusing on it~
10-Doing Great!

Listen to your Inner Critic

Mean girl vs. cheerleader

What does your "mean girl" say to you?
Start listening and blocking what she is saying....
Then replace it what what your "cheerleader" would say to you.

01 MEAN GIRL

02 CHEERLEADER

YOU DON'T HAVE CONTROL OVER WHAT OTHER PEOPLE SAY ABOUT YOU
BUT YOU HAVE 100% CONTROL OVER WHAT YOU SAY TO YOURSELF.
BE KIND!

Love the Woman in the Mirror

Don't Let the Inner Critic
Hold You Back
Clear Self-Limiting Beliefs
No Comparison
Practice Mirror Work

CHAPTER THREE

Love the Woman in the Mirror

SELF-LOVE FIRST

CLEAR LIMITING BELIEFS

CHANGE YOUR THOUGHTS TOWARD YOURSELF AND YOU WILL CHANGE YOUR LIFE

Step-By-Step Summary
Live your Fairy-Tale Life

1 Gain control of your triggers

2 Be mindful and present

3 Honor your values

4 Establish healthy boundaries

Manage Negative triggers + honor your values and Boundaries = Your Best Life

1. Who is draining your energy or who are you allowing to treat you in a way less than you deserve?

2. What are you spending time on that doesn't make you happy?

3. What do you need to say no to in your life?

4. What are you tolerating that isn't serving you?

5. What boundary do you need to honor so that others will also honor it?

> # Boundary Need Indicator

If someone ignores or fights you because you've set boundaries, that's just further evidence that the boundaries are indeed justified.

Tips for Boundary Success

- Get clear about what needs to change.
- Set boundaries for your own well-being not to control others.
- Be direct and don't apologize for your needs.
- Don't let resistance from people you say no to pressure you.
- You can't change everything overnight. Start with the areas that impact you most.
- Healthy boundaries weed out bad relationships; Let them go!
- Don't allow fear or lack to control your choices. Do what's best for you.
- Honor your own boundaries if you expect others to honor them, as well.
- Setting boundaries for your life will give you the foundation, time, resources and energy to thrive and pursue your best life.

HEALTHY BOUNDARIES

PROTECT YOUR ENERGY

Living the life you dream of starts with establishing boundaries in your life today. Protecting your energy is critical.

If you are always jumping through hoops for people to keep everyone happy or over-committing yourself to a point that you are stressed out and overwhelmed then you most likely have a boundary issue.

Not only do you have a maximum of twenty-four hours in a day but you also have a finite amount of energy to expend.

AN ABSENCE OF BOUNDARIES CAUSES YOU TO BE BITTER AND RESENTFUL

I'm going to give you some straight talk right now and it can be a difficult piece of truth to swallow...YOU MAY BE THE PROBLEM.

If you hate your work, can't get along with people, and feel stuck then you need to stop tolerating the life you've created and take control.

Stop automatically saying yes or simply agreeing to keep the peace. When someone asks something of you, if you can't do it with your whole heart and it's not a "Hell yes!", then it has to be a hard no.

Start practicing your no. It may feel uncomfortable at first but it will set you free and put you on course for your dreamed life. At a minimum, say "Let me think about that and I'll get back to you." It's easy enough to do and gives you time to really decide what is best for you.

You can gently say no to time-sucking requests by saying, "I cannot do that in a way that will best serve you or myself so I need to say no."

No one else can establish or uphold your boundaries. You must take a long hard look at your life and decide affirmatively what must change.

> *Envision a threshold that separates the essence of your being, the whispers of your mind, and the melody of your heart from those of the world around you. This safeguards your treasures, aspirations, and commitments.*

VALUE ASSESSMENT

Value conflicts can prevent you from living your best life and achieving your goals in relationships, business, and happiness.

01 WHAT ARE YOUR TOP FIVE VALUES?

02 WHICH VALUES ARE BEING VIOLATED IN YOUR LIFE?

03 WHAT DO YOU NEED TO DO TO HONOR YOUR VALUES?

HONOR YOUR VALUES

Address conflicts with core values

Most internal and external CONFLICTS stem from a violation of your core values. Values include:

Values you have that are not listed here:

Authenticity	Growth	Purpose
Achievement	Happiness	Recognition
Adventure	Honesty	Religion
Authority	Humor	Reputation
Balance	Independence	Respect
Beauty	Influence	Responsibility
Boldness	Inspiration	Security
Bravery	Integrity	Self-Respect
Belonging	Joy	Service
Compassion	Justice	Spirituality
Challenge	Kindness	Stability
Citizenship	Knowledge	Strength
Community	Leadership	Success
Calling	Learning	Status
Competency	Love	Trust
Contribution	Loyalty	Wealth
Creativity	Luxury	Wisdom
Determination	Meaning	
Experience	Openness	
Fairness	Peace	
Faith	Philanthropy	
Family	Pleasure	
Financial	Poise	
Freedom	Playfulness	
Friendship	Popularity	
Fun		

THE POWER OF PRESENCE

What are the benefits of being more present in your life?

Activities you will commit to with the objective of being more present

THE QUEEN'S COMPANION BOOK
BE MINDFUL AND PRESENT

Focusing on a future you cannot control prompts anxiety. Depression is activated when you are living in the past. How do you remedy this?

Wake up and be mindful and present everyday. Commit to implementing more of these activities and practice the power of being present.

Go Outside
- Explore in nature
- Walk somewhere new
- Bask in the sun
- Sit or walk in silence
- Play with your child

Move
- Exercise
- Take a dance class
- Ride a bike
- Walk and play with a pet
- Take up gardening
- Learn a sport

Play
- Games
- Act Silly
- Sing
- Dance
- Pretend
- Splash in the pool

Savor Everything
- Slow down
- Disconnect from technology
- Practice mindfulness, breathing
- Enjoy the view, take it all in
- Really taste your food, every bite
- Be truly present with everyone you encounter

BRIDGE THE GAP BETWEEN
REALITY AND YOUR IMAGINATION

YOU ARE ENOUGH

Three areas of my life that I don't feel like I am enough are:

01 What would being enought look like?

02 What action would I need to take to get from where I am to where I want to be?

03 What must I start doing to have my fairy-tale life?

04 What must I stop doing to have my fairy-tale life?

INVENTORY OF YOUR TRIGGERS

01
TRIGGERS

02
THOUGHTS

03
FEELINGS

04
REACTIONS

GAIN CONTROL

An emotional trigger is a sudden (undesired) reaction to something that happens evoking a strong emotion. It doesn't have anything to do with the specific situation.

Your brain is programmed to keep you safe. The emotional trigger often draws you into your past experiences where you have had a strong and negative response. Some examples of past experiences that can activate these are perceived failure, rejection, isolation, condemnation, shame, criticism, helplessness, an absence of control and being left out.

Triggers remind you of emotional pain or suffering from your childhood or past experiences, which then spark old thoughts, feelings, and behaviors to arise.

- TRIGGERS CREATE THOUGHTS
- THOUGHTS CREATE FEELINGS
- FEELINGS DIRECT ACTIONS
- ACTIONS CREATE YOUR LIFE

LIVE YOUR FAIRY-TALE LIFE

Manage Depression, Anxiety, and Expectations
Take Control of Your Life
Power of Presence
Close the Gap between Reality and Your Dreams

CHAPTER TWO

Live Your Fairy-Tale Life

MANAGE ANXIETY

DEPRESSION & EXPECTATIONS

MANAGING DEPRESSION, ANXIETY, AND EXPECTATIONS TO FEEL FREE AND PEACEFUL

STEP BY STEP SUMMARY
OWN YOUR POWER

1 ASSESS YOUR ZONE OF ABILITY TO DISCOVER AND KNOW YOUR PURPOSE

2 ACKNOWLEDGE PRIOR PAIN AND CREATE A PURPOSE FROM IT

3 IMPLEMENT YOUR PURPOSE WITH A PLAN

4 ANALYZE AND BUILD YOUR CONFIDENCE

PURPOSE + CONFIDENCE = POWER

Confidence and Power are directly connected

How to build Confidence

Self-Confidence is primarily Self-Acceptance

Confidence is built by:
- Doing things repetitively so that you get into the flow and build memory muscle;
- Being in alignment with who God created you to be so that your unique power is activated;
- Taking action and acknowledging small WINS along the way to your big goals;
- Being kind to yourself and affirming yourself;
- Establishing healthy boundaries; and
- Receiving positive feedback from others by surrounding yourself with encouraging people.

Confidence Analysis

Confidence is not found. Confidence is developed.

> What makes you great?

> What makes you feel your most confident?

STARTING TODAY
PURPOSE IMPLEMENTATION

ACTION PLAN

30 DAYS

ACTION PLAN

60 DAYS

ACTION PLAN

90 DAYS

KNOW YOUR PURPOSE

MY DREAM IS...

WHAT DO YOU DESIRE TO BE?	WHAT ARE YOUR TALENTS?

WHAT DID YOU LIKE TO DO AS A YOUNG GIRL?	IF YOU COULD DO ANYTHING, WHAT WOULD IT BE?

WHAT ARE YOUR TALENTS?	WHAT ARE YOUR PASSIONS?

> "Your purpose in life is to find your purpose and give your whole heart and soul to it"
> — Buddha

From Pain to Purpose

Everything you have endured can be used for GOOD!

What are three of your most difficult experiences?

What did you learn from these experiences?

How can you serve others based on what you overcame?

What can you teach others from what you learned from those experiences?

POWER ASSESSMENT
DISCOVER YOUR POWER (GENIUS) ZONE

WHAT DO OTHERS SAY YOU'RE GOOD AT DOING?	
WHAT DO YOU ENJOY DOING FOR FREE?	
AT WHAT DO YOU EXCEL?	
WHAT COULD YOU DO EVERYDAY?	
WHAT IS IN YOUR SKILL ZONE THAT YOU DON'T ENJOY DOING?	
WHAT DO YOU THINK YOUR POWERS ARE?	

The Power and Ability Connection

Three Zones of Ability

Power Zone - Skill Zone - Weakness Zone

You can build a skill in anything but you should focus on your Power (Genius) Zone! Working only in the area of your Skill Zone will keep you small and struggling.

Your Power (Genius) Zone	Your Weakness Zone
Is Effortless;	Leaves you Exhausted;
Focused;	Unmotivated;
Energizing;	Overwhelmed;
Satisfying; and	Inefficient; and

OWN YOUR POWER

Discover Your Purpose
Know Your Purpose
Increase Your Confidence

CHAPTER ONE

Own Your Power

BE POWERFUL!

BE YOU!

STEP INTO YOUR PURPOSE AND CONFIDENCE TO ELEVATE YOUR POWER

A QUEEN'S TWELVE STEPS

01 — OWN YOUR POWER

02 — LIVE YOUR FAIRY-TALE LIFE

03 — LOVE THE WOMAN IN THE MIRROR

04 — ACCEPT YOUR TITLE

05 — PROCLAIM YOUR GRACE

06 — SEIZE YOUR SHIELD OF SATISFACTION

07 — REIGN YOURSELF

08 — FORTRESS OF COPING

09 — RICHES ARE YOUR BIRTHRIGHT

10 — TOWER OF HEALTH

11 — RELATIONSHIP REALM

12 — WORTH MORE THAN GOLD

TABLE OF CONTENTS

11	RELATIONSHIP REALM	153
12	WORTH MORE THAN GOLD	175
13	CONCLUSION: CORONATION OF A QUEEN	199
14	CHECKLIST	205
15	RESOURCES	209

TABLE OF CONTENTS

06	Seize your shield of satisfaction	71
07	Reign Yourself	85
08	Fortress of Coping	107
09	Riches are your Birthright	123
10	Tower of Health	143

TABLE OF CONTENTS

01 Own Your Power 1

02 Live your Fairy-tale Life 15

03 Love the Woman in the Mirror 31

04 Accept your title 43

05 Proclaim Grace 55

xv

WHAT'S INSIDE WAITING FOR YOU

The 12 steps included in this book are developed by Author-Speaker-Coach, Nicole B. Gebhardt, sharing unlocking techniques, secrets, and guidance for a fulfilled life and career. *The Queen's Companion Book: Rule Your Throne. Own Your Queendom* is an unprecedented and comprehensive program that provides detailed insight on how to take charge of your life and direct your own destiny, professionally and personally.

Supported by a focus group of over 2000 women, this book uses the same methodology that the author implemented in transforming and triumphing in her own life, as well as with her coaching clients in theirs.

THE QUEEN'S COMPANION BOOK

Unlock the Secrets to:

IDENTITY

EMPOWERMENT

WORTHINESS

QUEENS: GREETINGS!

I had a childhood of molestation and rape, years of depression, an abusive marriage, and the death of a child. I suffered from low self-esteem, never feeling good enough, and floundering in my identity and purpose.

Through a fateful and almost fatal fall down the stairs, I began a journey of discovery and evolution that led me to overcome grief, addiction, and unworthiness. Shaking off the victim persona and not wanting to accept the title of survivor, I struggled and ultimately rose to find my purpose as a "Bad-Ass Queen." I'm happier than ever, have a prince of a husband, amazing children and live my passion as a coach, Reiki Master, author, speaker and empower women worldwide. I crafted this workbook-like companion as an accompaniment to my memoir, *A Queen Saves Herself: A Story of Transformation and Triumph*, especially for you. I did so, because after hearing my story, so many women asked how I came out on the other side of glory after sustaining such unfathomable traumas and tragedies.

This is my gift to you: A must-read for any woman looking for strength, renewal, hope, and inspiration. Know you deserve the life you've dreamed of and are worthy to claim it.

Nicole B. Gebhardt

IN EVERY WOMAN,
THERE IS A QUEEN.

SPEAK TO THE
QUEEN AND THE
QUEEN WILL
ANSWER.

Norwegian Proverb

To the Women who don't feel seen
or heard:

You have yet to tap into your power.

This is for You.

You are worthy. You are enough.

You have the courage to overcome.

You have the gifts to fulfill your
dreams.

YOU ARE A QUEEN

"There's no prerequisites to worthiness. You're born worthy. And that's a message a lot of women need to hear."

—Viola Davis

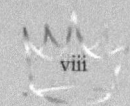

RULE YOUR THRONE: OWN YOUR QUEENDOM

THE QUEEN'S
COMPANION BOOK

THE 12 STEPS

PROVEN AND SUPPORTED BY
A FOCUS GROUP OF
OVER 2000 WOMEN

NICOLE B. GEBHARDT

This book is for informational purposes only. It is not intended to serve as a substitute for professional psychological or medical advice. The author and publisher disclaim any and all liability arising directly or indirectly from the use of any information contained in this book. A healthcare professional should be consulted regarding your specific psychological or medical situation.

The Queen's Companion Book: Rule Your Throne. Own Your Queendom,
Copyright @ 2023 by Nicole B. Gebhardt

All rights reserved. No part of this book may be used or reproduced in any manner whatsoever without written permission of the publisher.

SILVERLIGHT PRESS

Silverlight Press
P.O. Box 342544
Austin, Texas 78734
ThroughPenandLens.com
Printed in the United States of America

ISBN
979-8-9877050-7-0 - Hardbound
979-8-9877050-8-7 Paperback

Cover Design by Randy Goad
Photography of Nicole B. Gebhardt by Monica L. Hagen
Publisher Susan Sember, Silverlight Press
Copyright 2023. All Rights Reserved.

10 9 8 7 6 5 4 3 2 1

Special discounts for bulk sales are available.
Please contact bulkorders@throughpenandlens.com

THE QUEEN'S

COMPANION BOOK

NICOLE B. GEBHARDT

THE QUEEN'S
COMPANION BOOK
TESTIMONIALS AND PRAISE

ASHLEY J.

This is the most comprehensive personal development book I've ever read. It prompted me to self-reflect like never before. Amazing, thought-provoking, and empowering content.

RENE V.

As I was reading and answering the prompts from Nicole, I felt like she was right there guiding me and cheering me on! Thank you Nicole for your support in this woman's journey.

SANDI O.

The only next best thing to this book would be to have Nicole coach me in person! Never had a "workbook" of such quality and value. Worth the investment and time.

JENNIFER S.

I thought as an established professional, wife, and mother, I would never find a "workbook" that taught me something I hadn't read or heard already. WRONG! This one defied that belief. A great go-to resource.

NICOLEBGEBHARDT.COM

THE QUEEN'S
COMPANION BOOK

THE 12 STEPS PROVEN AND SUPPORTED BY A FOCUS GROUP OF OVER 2,000 WOMEN

Rule Your Throne: Own Your Queendom

NICOLE B. GEBHARDT